AMERICAN NATIONAL POLITICAL INSTITUTIONS

Some Key Readings

Edited and Notes By

WILLIAM G. ANDREWS

Tufts University

D. VAN NOSTRAND COMPANY, INC.

Princeton, New Jersey

Toronto London

New York

TO
MY PARENTS

D. VAN NOSTRAND COMPANY, INC.
120 Alexander St., Princeton, New Jersey (*Principal office*); 24 West 40 St., New York, N.Y.
D. VAN NOSTRAND COMPANY (Canada), LTD.
25 Hollinger Rd., Toronto 16, Canada
D. VAN NOSTRAND COMPANY, LTD.
358, Kensington High Street, London, W.14, England

Published simultaneously in Canada by
D. Van Nostrand Company (Canada), Ltd.

PRINTED IN THE UNITED STATES OF AMERICA

PREFACE

This short collection of readings in American government has two aims: 1) to provide in convenient form a few "core" outside readings that will permit diversification of students' reading assignments in survey courses even where limits on time and means preclude use of a more comprehensive collection. 2) To complement a forthcoming larger collection of readings on the British, French, German, and Soviet governments.

The principle guiding the selection of readings on the foreign governments was that of choosing, as far as possible, material that provides subjective views of the governments by high level participants or illustrative material on the operation of the institutions. Most of the readings included here fall into those categories also. I adopted them in the belief that effective supplementary material sharpens the student's perception best by providing him with views from different perspectives. To complement the objective, descriptive material of textbook and lecture, these readings present subjective and illustrative material.

Some "classic" writings have been added here. Tocqueville's short chapter on popular sovereignty has been chosen as a classic pronouncement on the principle of American democracy and two contributions to the debate over the character of American parties were picked as a useful focus for any discussion of that lively, contemporary issue. Most of the selections that fit the first criterion are also classics. The Supreme Court opinions all support key decisions, the Federalist essays are unrivalled in American constitutional theory, and the Taft-Roosevelt views on the power of the Presidency are standard statements on that question.

The determination of criteria did not obviate the selection of items. A collection of *the* key readings on American national political institutions "would partake of the prolixity of a legal code." I am merely presenting *some* key readings. In arriving at my decisions I received very helpful suggestions from Professors Elmer Smead and Franklin Smallwood of Dartmouth College, Robert R. Robbins of Tufts University, and Franklin L. Burdette of the University of Maryland. They will detect the marks of their influence. There was and inevitably will be disagreement with my decisions. I will greatly appreciate suggestions from colleagues concerning revisions that might be made if this collection has sufficient appeal to warrant reprinting.

Mrs. Geraldine McCarthy, Miss Lucille Flanders, and Mrs. Edna Nelson deserve my gratitude for their typing services and my wife assisted me in proofreading. The American Political Science Assn., Charles Scribner's Sons, and the Columbia University Press kindly granted permission to use material for which they hold copyright.

Belmont, Massachusetts WILLIAM G. ANDREWS
July, 1961

TABLE OF CONTENTS

— 1

FUNDAMENTAL PRINCIPLES

Between October 1787 and May 1788 a series of eighty-five essays signed "Publius" appeared, mostly in the newspapers of New York State, advocating ratification of the proposed federal Constitution. Three members of the Philadelphia Convention that drafted the Constitution were the authors. Alexander Hamilton wrote fifty-one, James Madison wrote fourteen, and John Jay wrote five of the essays. Hamilton and Madison collaborated on three and there is uncertainty whether Hamilton or Madison was the author of the remaining twelve.

The essays were reprinted widely at the time and were published in book form in 1788. They have since acquired a reputation as one of the few significant American contributions to political theory.

Probably no work is a better guide to the intentions of the Founders of the American Republic. It is the most literate, articulate, and, despite its multiple authorship and periodical character, the most systematic explanation of the Constitution by members of the drafting convention. For this reason, coupled with the continuing influence of the Constitution on the operation of the American system, several of the more important Federalist papers treating principles that still lie at the foundation of our regime are included here.

FEDERALIST NO. 10

By James Madison

Federalist No. 10 was first published in the New York Packet, *November 23, 1787.*

Among the numerous advantages promised by a well-constructed Union, none deserves to be more accurately developed than its tendency to break and control the violence of faction. The friend of popular governments never finds himself so much alarmed for their character and fate, as when he contemplates their propensity to this dangerous vice. He will not fail, therefore, to set a due value on any plan which, without violating the principles to which he is attached, provides a proper cure for it. The instability, injustice, and confusion introduced into the public councils, have, in truth, been the mortal diseases under which popular governments have everywhere perished; as they continue to be the favorite and fruitful topics from which the adversaries to liberty derive their most specious declamations. The valuable improvements made by the American constitutions on the popular models, both ancient and modern, cannot certainly be too much admired; but it would be an unwarrantable partiality, to contend that they have as effectually obviated the danger on this side, as was wished and expected. Complaints are everywhere heard from our most considerate and virtuous citizens, equally the friends of public and private faith, and of public and personal liberty, that our governments are too unstable, that the public good is disregarded in the conflicts of rival parties, and that measures are too often decided, not according to the rules of justice and the rights of the minor party, but by the superior force of an interested and overbearing majority. However anxiously we may wish that these complaints had no foundation, the evidence of known facts will not permit us to deny that they are in some degree true. It will be found, indeed, on a candid review of our situation, that some of the distresses under which we labor have been erroneously charged on the operation of our governments; but it will be found, at the same time, that other causes will not alone account for many of our heaviest misfortunes; and, particularly, for that prevailing and increasing distrust of public engagements, and alarm for private rights, which are echoed from one end of the continent to the other. These must be chiefly, if not wholly, effects of the unsteadiness and injustice with which a factious spirit has tainted our public administrations.

By a faction, I understand a number of citizens, whether amounting to a majority or minority of the whole, who are united and actuated by some common impulse of passion, or of interest, adverse to the rights of other citizens, or to the permanent and aggregate interests of the community.

There are two methods of curing the mischiefs of faction: the one, by removing its causes; the other, by controlling its effects.

There are again two methods of removing the causes of faction: the one, by destroying the liberty which is essential to its existence; the other, by giving to every citizen the same opinions, the same passions, and the same interests.

It could never be more truly said than of the first remedy, that it was worse than the disease. Liberty is to faction what air is to fire, an aliment without which it instantly expires. But it could not be less folly to abolish liberty, which is essential to political life, because it nourishes faction, than it would be to wish the annihilation of air, which is essential to animal life, because it imparts to fire its destructive agency.

The second expedient is as impracticable as the first would be unwise. As long as the reason of man continues fallible, and he is at liberty to exercise it, different opinions will be formed. As long as the connection subsists between his reason and his self-love, his opinions and his passions will have a reciprocal influence on each other: and the former will be objects to which the latter will attach themselves. The diversity in the faculties of men, from which the rights of property originate, is not less an insuperable obstacle to a uniformity of interests. The protection of these faculties is the first object of government. From the protection of different and unequal faculties of acquiring property, the possession of different degrees and kinds of property immediately results; and from the influence of these on the sentiments and views of the respective proprietors, ensues a division of the society into different interests and parties.

The latent causes of faction are thus sown in the nature of man; and we see them everywhere brought into different degrees of activity, according to the different circumstances of civil society. A zeal for different opinions concerning religion, concerning government, and many other points, as well of speculation as of practice; an attachment to different leaders ambitiously contending for pre-eminence and power; or to persons of other descriptions whose fortunes have been interesting to the human passions, have, in turn, divided mankind into parties, inflamed them with mutual animosity, and rendered them much more disposed to vex and oppress each other than to co-operate for their common good. So strong is this propensity of mankind to fall into mutual animosities, that where no substantial occasion presents itself, the most frivolous and fanciful distinctions have been sufficient to kindle their unfriendly passions and excite their most violent conflicts. But the most common and durable source of factions has been the various and unequal distribution of property. Those who hold and those who are without property have ever formed distinct interests in society. Those who are creditors, and those who are debtors, fall under a like discrimination. A landed interest, a manufacturing interest, a mercantile interest, a moneyed interest, with many lesser interests, grow up of necessity in civilized nations, and divide them into different classes, actuated by different sentiments and views. The regulation of these various and interfering interests forms the principal task of modern legislation, and involves the spirit of party and faction in the necessary and ordinary operations of the government.

No man is allowed to be a judge in his own cause, because his interest would certainly bias his judgment, and, not improbably, corrupt his integrity. With equal, nay with greater reason, a body of men are unfit to be both judges and parties at the same time; yet what are many of the most important acts of legislation, but so many judicial determinations, not indeed concerning the rights of single persons, but concerning the rights of large bodies of citizens? And what are the different classes of legislators but advocates and parties to the causes which they determine? Is a law proposed concerning private debts? It is a question to which the creditors are parties on one side and the debtors on the other. Justice ought to hold the balance between them. Yet the parties are, and must be, themselves the judges; and the most numerous party, or, in other words, the most powerful faction must be expected to prevail. Shall domestic manufactures be encouraged, and in what degree, by restrictions on foreign manufactures? are questions which would be differently decided by the landed and the manufacturing classes, and probably by neither with a sole regard to justice and the public good. The apportionment of taxes on the various descriptions of property is an act which seems to require the most exact impartiality; yet there is, perhaps, no legislative act in which greater opportunity and temptation are given to a predominant party to trample on the rules of justice. Every shilling with which they overburden the inferior number, is a shilling saved to their own pockets.

It is in vain to say that enlightened statesmen will be able to adjust these clashing interests, and render them all subservient to the public good. Enlightened statesmen will not always be at the helm. Nor, in many cases, can such an adjustment be made at all without taking into view indirect and remote considerations, which will rarely prevail over the immediate interest which one party may find in disregarding the rights of another or the good of the whole.

The inference to which we are brought is, that the *causes* of faction cannot be removed, and that relief is only to be sought in the means of controlling its *effects*.

If a faction consists of less than a majority, relief is supplied by the republican principle, which enables the majority to defeat its sinister views by regular vote. It may clog the administration, it may convulse the society; but it will be unable to execute and mask its violence under the forms of the Constitution. When a majority is included in a faction, the form of popular government, on the other hand, enables it to sacrifice to its ruling passion or interest both the public good and the rights of other citizens. To secure the public good and private rights against the danger of such a faction, and at the same time to preserve the spirit and the form of popular government, is then the great object to which our inquiries are directed. Let me add that it is the great desideratum by which this form of government can be rescued from the opprobrium under which it has so long labored, and be recommended to the esteem and adoption of mankind.

By what means is this object attainable? Evidently by one of two only. Either the existence of the same passion or interest in a majority at the same time must be prevented, or the majority, having such coexistent passion or interest, must be rendered, by their number and local situation, unable to concert and carry into effect schemes of oppression. If the impulse and the opportunity be suffered to coincide, we well know that neither moral nor religious motives can be relied on as an adequate control. They are not found to be such on the injustice and violence of individuals, and lose their efficacy in proportion to the number combined together, that is, in proportion as their efficacy becomes needful.

From this view of the subject it may be concluded that a pure democracy, by which I mean a society consisting of a small number of citizens, who assemble and administer the government in person, can admit of no cure for the mischiefs of faction. A common passion or interest will, in almost every case, be felt by a majority of the whole; a communication and concert result from the form of government itself; and there is nothing to check the inducements to sacrifice the weaker party or an obnoxious individual. Hence it is that such democracies have ever been spectacles of turbulence and contention; have ever been found incompatible with personal security or the rights of property; and have in general been as short in their lives as they have been violent in their deaths. Theoretic politicians, who have patronized this species of government, have erroneously supposed that by reducing mankind to a perfect equality in their political rights, they would, at the same time, be perfectly equalized and assimilated in their possessions, their opinions, and their passions.

A republic, by which I mean a government in which the scheme of representation takes place, opens a different prospect, and promises the cure for which we are seeking. Let us examine the points in which it varies from pure democracy, and we shall comprehend both the nature of the cure and the efficacy which it must derive from the Union.

The two great points of difference between a democracy and a republic are: first, the delegation of the government, in the latter, to a small number of citizens elected by the rest; secondly, the greater number of citizens, and greater sphere of country, over which the latter may be extended.

The effect of the first difference is, on the one hand, to refine and enlarge the public views, by passing them through the medium of a chosen body of citizens, whose wisdom may best discern the true interest of their country, and whose patriotism and love of justice will be least likely to sacrifice it to temporary or partial considerations. Under such a regulation, it may well happen that the public voice, pronounced by the representatives of the people, will be more consonant to the public good than if pronounced by the people themselves, convened for the purpose. On the other hand, the effect may be inverted. Men of factious tempers, of local prejudices, or of sinister designs, may, by intrigue, by corruption, or by other means, first obtain the suffrages, and then betray the interests, of the people. The question resulting is, whether small or extensive republics are more favorable to the election of proper guardians of the public weal; and it is clearly decided in favor of the latter by two obvious considerations:

In the first place, it is to be remarked that, however small the republic may be, the representatives must be raised to a certain number, in order to guard against the cabals of a few; and that, however large it may be, they must be limited to a certain number, in order to guard against the confusion of a multitude. Hence, the number of representatives in the two cases not being in proportion to that of the two constituents, and being proportionally greater in the small republic, it follows that, if the proportion of fit characters be not less in the large than in the small republic, the former will present a greater option, and consequently a greater probability of a fit choice.

In the next place, as each representative will be chosen by a greater number of citizens in the large than in the small republic, it will be more difficult for unworthy candidates to practise with success the vicious arts by which elections are too often carried; and the suffrages of the people being more free, will be more likely to centre in men who possess the most attractive merit and the most diffusive and established characters.

It must be confessed that in this, as in most other cases, there is a mean, on both sides of which inconveniences will be found to lie. By enlarging too much the number of electors, you render the representative too little acquainted with all their local circumstances and lesser interests; as by reducing it too much, you render him unduly attached to these, and too little fit to comprehend and pursue great and national objects. The federal Constitution forms a happy combination in this respect; the great and aggregate interests being referred to the national, the local and particular to the State legislatures.

The other point of difference is, the greater number of citizens and extent of territory which may be brought within the compass of republican than of democratic government; and it is this circumstance principally which renders factious combinations less to be dreaded in the former than in the latter. The smaller the society, the fewer probably will be the distinct parties and interests composing it; the fewer the distinct parties and interests, the more frequently will a majority be found of the same party; and the smaller the number of individuals composing a majority, and the smaller the compass within which they are placed, the more easily will they concert and execute their plans of oppression. Extend the sphere, and you take in a greater variety of parties and interests; you make it less probable that a majority of the whole will have a common motive to invade the rights of other citizens; or if such a common motive exists, it will be more difficult for all who feel it to discover their own strength, and to act in unison with each other. Besides other impediments, it may be remarked that, where there is a consciousness of unjust or dishonorable purposes, communication is always checked by distrust in proportion to the number whose concurrence is necessary.

Hence, it clearly appears, that the same advantage which a republic has over a democracy, in controlling the effects of faction, is enjoyed by a large over a small republic,—is enjoyed by the Union over the States composing it. Does the advantage consist in the substitution of representatives whose enlightened views and virtuous sentiments render them superior to local prejudices and to schemes of injustice? It will not be denied that the representation of the Union will be most likely to possess these requisite endowments. Does it consist in the greater security afforded by a greater variety of parties, against the event of any one party being able to outnumber and oppress the rest? In an equal degree does the increased variety of parties comprised within the Union, increase this security. Does it, in fine, consist in the greater obstacles opposed to the concert and accomplishment of the secret wishes of an unjust and interested majority? Here, again, the extent of the Union gives it the most palpable advantage.

The influence of factious leaders may kindle a flame within their particular States, but will be unable to spread a general conflagration through the other States. A religious sect may degenerate into a political faction in a part of the Confederacy; but the variety of sects dispersed over the entire face of it must secure the national councils against any danger from that source. A rage for paper money, for an abolition of debts, for an equal division of property, or for any other improper or wicked project, will be less apt to pervade the whole body of the Union than a particular member of it; in the same proportion as such a malady is more likely to taint a particular county or district, than an entire State.

In the extent and proper structure of the Union, therefore, we behold a republican remedy for the diseases most incident to republican government. And according to the degree of pleasure and pride we feel in being republicans, ought to be our zeal in cherishing the spirit and supporting the character of Federalists. PUBLIUS

FEDERALIST NO. 47

By James Madison

This essay was first published in the New York Packet *on February 1, 1788.*

Having reviewed the general form of the proposed government and the general mass of power allotted to it, I proceed to examine the particular structure of this government, and the distribution of this mass of power among its constituent parts.

One of the principal objections inculcated by the more respectable adversaries to the Constitution, is its supposed violation of the political maxim, that the legislative, executive, and judiciary departments ought to be separate and distinct. In the structure of the federal government, no regard, it is said, seems to have been paid to this essential precaution in favor of liberty. The several departments of power are distributed and blended in such a manner as at once to destroy all symmetry and beauty of form, and to expose some of the essential parts of the edifice to the danger of being crushed by the disproportionate weight of other parts.

No political truth is certainly of greater intrinsic value, or is stamped with the authority of more enlightened patrons of liberty, than that on which the objection is founded. The accumulation of all powers, legislative, executive, and judiciary, in the same hands, whether of one, a few, or many, and whether hereditary, self-appointed, or elective, may justly be pronounced the very definition of tyranny. Were the federal Constitution, therefore, really chargeable with the accumulation of power, or with a mixture of powers, having a dangerous tendency to such an accumulation, no further arguments would be necessary to inspire a universal reprobation of the system. I persuade myself, however, that it will be made apparent to every one, that the charge cannot be supported, and that the maxim on which it relies has been totally misconceived and misapplied. In order to form correct ideas on this important subject, it will be proper to investigate the sense in which the preservation of liberty requires that the three great departments of power should be separate and distinct.

The oracle who is always consulted and cited on this subject is the celebrated Montesquieu. If he be not the author of this invaluable precept in the science of politics, he has the merit at least of displaying and recommending it most effectually to the attention of mankind. Let us endeavor, in the first place, to ascertain his meaning on this point.

The British Constitution was to Montesquieu what Homer has been to the didactic writers on epic poetry. As the latter have considered the work of the immortal bard as the perfect model from which the principles and rules of the epic art were to be drawn, and by which all similar works were to be judged, so this great political critic appears to have viewed the Constitution of England as the standard, or to use his own expression, as the mirror of political liberty; and to have delivered, in the form of elementary truths, the several characteristic principles of that particular system. That we may be sure, then, not to mistake his meaning in this case, let us recur to the source from which the maxim was drawn.

On the slightest view of the British Constitution, we must perceive that the legislative, executive, and judiciary departments are by no means totally separate and distinct from each other. The executive magistrate forms an integral part of the legislative authority. He alone has the prerogative of making treaties with foreign sovereigns, which, when made, have, under certain limitations, the force of legislative acts. All the members of the judiciary department are appointed by him, can be removed by him on the address of the two Houses of Parliament, and form, when he pleases to consult them, one of his constitutional councils. One branch of the legislative department forms also a great constitutional council to the executive chief, as, on another hand, it is the sole depository of judicial power in cases of impeachment, and is invested with the supreme appellate jurisdiction in all other cases. The judges, again, are so far connected with the legislative department as often to attend and participate in its deliberations, though not admitted to a legislative vote.

From these facts, by which Montesquieu was guided, it may clearly be inferred that, in saying "There can be no liberty where the legislative and executive powers are united in the same person, or body of magistrates," or, "if the power of judging be not separated from the legislative and executive powers," he did not mean that these departments ought to have no *partial agency* in, or no *control* over, the acts of each other. His meaning, as his own words import, and still more conclusively as illustrated by the example in his eye, can amount to no more than this, that where the *whole* power of one department is exercised by the same hands which possess the *whole* power of another department, the fundamental principles of a free constitution are subverted. This would have been the case in the constitution examined by him, if the king, who is the sole executive magistrate, had possessed also the complete legislative power, or the supreme administration of justice; or if the entire legislative body had possessed the supreme judiciary, or the supreme executive authority. This, however is not among the vices of that constitution. The magistrate in whom the whole executive power resides cannot of himself make a law, though he can put a negative on every law; nor administer justice in person, though he has the appointment of those who do administer it. The judges can exercise no executive prerogative, though they are shoots from the executive stock; nor any legislative function, though they may be advised with by the legislative councils. The entire legislature can perform no judiciary act, though by the joint act of two of its branches the judges may be removed from their offices, and though one of its branches is possessed of the judicial power in the last resort. The entire legislature, again, can exercise no executive prerogative, though one of its branches constitutes the supreme executive magistracy, and another, on the impeachment of a third, can try and condemn all the subordinate officers in the executive department.

The reasons on which Montesquieu grounds his maxim are a further demonstration of his meaning. "When the legislative and executive powers are united in the same person or body," says he, "there can be no liberty, because apprehensions may arise lest *the same* monarch or senate should *enact* tyrannical laws to *execute* them in a tyrannical manner." Again: "Were the power of judging joined with the legislative, the life and liberty of the subject would be exposed to arbitrary control, for *the judge* would then be *the legislator.* Were it joined to the executive power, *the judge* might behave with all the violence of *an oppressor.*" Some of these reasons are more fully explained in other passages; but briefly stated as they are here, they sufficiently establish the meaning which we have put on this celebrated maxim of this celebrated author.

If we look into the constitutions of the several States, we find that, notwithstanding the emphatical and, in some instances, the unqualified terms in which this axiom has been laid down, there is not a single instance in which the several departments of power have been kept absolutely separate and distinct. New Hampshire, whose constitution was the last formed, seems to have been fully aware of the impossibility and inexpediency of avoiding any mixture whatever of these departments, and has qualified the doctrine by declaring "that the legislative, executive, and judiciary powers ought to be kept as separate from, and independent of, each other *as the nature of a free government will admit; or as is consistent with that chain of connection that binds the whole fabric of the constitution in one indissoluble bond of unity and amity.*" Her constitution accordingly mixes these departments in several respects. The Senate, which is a branch of the legislative department, is also a judicial tribunal for the trial of impeachments. The President, who is the head of the executive department, is the presiding member also of the Senate; and, besides an equal vote in all cases, has a casting vote in case of a tie. The executive head is himself eventually elective every year by the legislative department, and his council is every year chosen by and from the members of the same department. Several of the officers of state are also appointed by the legislature. And the members of the judiciary department are appointed by the executive department.

The constitution of Massachusetts has observed a sufficient though less pointed caution, in expressing this fundamental article of liberty. It declares "that the legislative departments shall never exercise the executive and judicial powers, or either of them; the executive shall never exercise the legislative and judicial powers, or either of them; the judicial shall never exercise the legislative and executive powers, or either of them." This declaration corresponds precisely with the doctrine of Montesquieu, as it has been explained, and is not in a single point violated by the plan of the convention. It goes no farther than to prohibit any one of the entire departments from exercising the powers of another department. In the very Constitution to which it is prefixed, a partial mixture of powers has been admitted. The executive magistrate has a qualified negative on the legislative body, and the Senate, which is a part of the legislature, is a court of impeachment for members both of the executive and judiciary departments. The members of the judiciary department, again, are appointable by the executive department, and removable by the same authority on the address of the two legislative branches. Lastly, a number of the officers of government are annually appointed by the legislative department. As the appointment to offices, particularly executive offices, is in its nature an executive function, the compilers of the Constitution have, in this last point at least, violated the rule established by themselves.

I pass over the constitutions of Rhode Island and Connecticut, because they were formed prior to the Revolution, and even before the principle under examination had become an object of political attention.

The constitution of New York contains no declaration on this subject; but appears very clearly to have been framed with an eye to the danger of improperly blending the different departments. It gives, nevertheless, to the executive magistrate, a partial control over the legislative department; and, what is more, gives a like control to the judiciary department; and even blends the executive and judiciary departments in the exercise of this control. In its council of appointment members of the legislative are associated with the executive authority, in the appointment of officers, both executive and judiciary. And its court for the trial of impeachments and correction of errors is to consist of one branch of the legislature and the principal members of the judiciary department.

The constitution of New Jersey has blended the different powers of government more than any of the preceding. The governor, who is the executive magistrate, is appointed by the legislature; is chancellor and ordinary, or surrogate of the State; is a member of the Supreme Court of Appeals, and president, with a casting vote, of one of the legislative branches. The same legislative branch acts again as executive council of the governor, and with him constitutes the Court of Appeals. The members of the judiciary department are appointed by the legislative department, and removable by one branch of it, on the impeachment of the other.

According to the constitution of Pennsylvania, the president, who is the head of the executive department, is annually elected by a vote in which the legislative department predominates. In conjunction with an executive council, he appoints the members of the judiciary department, and forms a court of impeachment for trial of all officers, judiciary as well as executive. The judges of the Supreme Court and justices of the peace seem also to be removable by the legislature; and the executive power of pardoning in certain cases, to be referred to the same department. The members of the executive council are made EX-OFFICIO justices of peace throughout the State.

In Delaware, the chief executive magistrate is annually elected by the legislative department. The speakers of the two legislative branches are vice-presidents in the executive department. The executive chief, with six others, appointed, three by each of the legislative branches, constitutes the Supreme Court of Appeals; he is joined with the legislative department in the appointment of the other judges. Throughout the States, it appears that the members of the legislature may at the same time be justices of the peace; in this State, the members of one branch of it are EX-OFFICIO justices of the peace; as are also the members of the executive council. The principal officers of the executive department are appointed by the legislative; and one branch of the latter forms a court of impeachments. All officers may be removed on address of the legislature.

Maryland has adopted the maxim in the most unqualified terms; declaring that the legislative, executive, and judicial powers of government ought to be forever separate and distinct from each other. Her constitution, notwithstanding, makes the executive magistrate appointable by the legislative department; and the members of the judiciary by the executive department.

The language of Virginia is still more pointed on this subject. Her constitution declares, "that the legislative, executive, and judiciary departments shall be separate and distinct; so that neither exercise the powers properly belonging to the other; nor shall any person exercise the powers of more than one of them at the same time, except that the justices of county courts shall be eligible to either House of Assembly." Yet we find not only this express exception, with respect to the members of the inferior courts, but that the chief magistrate, with his executive council, are appointable by the legislature; that two members of the latter are triennially displaced at the pleasure of the legislature; and that all the principal offices, both executive and judiciary, are filled by the same department. The executive prerogative of pardon, also, is in one case vested in the legislative department.

The constitution of North Carolina, which declares "that the legislative, executive, and supreme judicial powers of government ought to be forever separate and distinct from each other," refers, at the same time, to the legislative department, the appointment not only of the executive chief, but all the principal officers within both that and the judiciary department.

In South Carolina, the constitution makes the executive magistracy elegible by the legislative department. It gives to the latter, also, the appointment of the members of the judiciary department, including even justices of the peace and sheriffs; and the appointment of officers in the executive department, down to captains in the army and navy of the State.

In the constitution of Georgia, where it is declared "that the legislative, executive, and judiciary departments shall be separate and distinct, so that neither exercise the powers properly belonging to the other," we find that the executive department is to be filled by appointments of the legislature; and the executive prerogative of pardon to be finally exercised by the same authority. Even justices of the peace are to be appointed by the legislature.

In citing these cases, in which the legislative, executive, and judiciary departments have not been kept totally separate and distinct, I wish not to be regarded as an advocate for the particular organizations of the several State governments. I am fully aware that among the many excellent principles which they exemplify, they carry strong marks of the haste, and still stronger of the inexperience, under which they were framed. It is but too obvious that in some instances the fundamental principle under consideration has been violated by too great a mixture, and even an actual consolidation, of the different powers; and that in no instance has a competent provision been made for maintaining in practice the separation delineated on paper. What I have wished to evince is, that the charge brought against the proposed Constitution, of violating the sacred maxim of free government, is warranted neither by the real meaning annexed to that maxim by its author, nor by the sense in which it has hitherto been understood in America. This interesting subject will be resumed in the ensuing paper. PUBLIUS

FEDERALIST NO. 48

By James Madison

This essay first appeared in the New York Packet, *February 1, 1788.*

It was shown in the last paper that the political apothegm there examined does not require that the legislative, executive, and judiciary departments should be wholly unconnected with each other. I shall undertake, in the next place, to show that unless these departments be so far connected and blended as to give to each a constitutional control over the others, the degree of separation which the maxim requires, as essential to a free government, can never in practice be duly maintained.

It is agreed on all sides, that the powers properly belonging to one of the departments ought not to be directly and completely administered by either of the other departments. It is equally evident, that none of them ought to possess, directly or indirectly, an overruling influence over the others, in the administration of their respective powers. It will not be denied, that power is of an encroaching nature, and that it ought to be effectually restrained from passing the limits assigned to it. After discriminating, therefore, in theory, the several classes of power, as they may in their nature be legislative, executive, or judiciary, the next and most difficult task is to provide some practical security for each, against the invasion of the others. What this security ought to be, is the great problem to be solved.

Will it be sufficient to mark, with precision, the boundaries of these deparments, in the constitution of the government, and to trust to these parchment barriers against the encroaching spirit of power? This is the security which appears to have been principally relied on by the compilers of most of the American constitutions. But experience assures us, that the efficacy of the provision has been greatly overrated; and that some more adequate defence is indispensably necessary for the more feeble, against the more powerful, members of the government. The legislative department is everywhere extending the sphere of its activity, and drawing all power into its impetuous vortex.

The founders of our republics have so much merit for the wisdom which they have displayed, that no task can be less pleasing than that of pointing out the errors into which they have fallen. A respect for truth, however, obliges us to remark, that they seem never for a moment to have turned their eyes from the danger to liberty from the overgrown and all-grasping prerogative of an hereditary magistrate, supported and fortified by an hereditary branch of the legislative authority. They seem never to have recollected the danger from legislative usurpations, which, by assembling all power in the same hands, must lead to the same tyranny as is threatened by executive usurpations.

In a government where numerous and extensive prerogatives are placed in the hands of an hereditary monarch, the executive department is very justly regarded as the source of danger, and watched with all the jealousy which a zeal for liberty ought to inspire. In a democracy, where a multitude of people exercise in person the legislative functions, and are continually exposed, by their incapacity for regular deliberation and concerted measures, to the ambitious intrigues of their executive magistrates, tyranny may well be apprehended, on some favorable emergency, to start up in the same quarter. But in a representative republic, where the executive magistracy is carefully limited, both in the extent and the duration of its power; and where the legislative power is exercised by an assembly, which is inspired, by a supposed influence over the people, with an intrepid confidence in its own strength; which is sufficiently numerous to feel all the passions which actuate a multitude, yet not so numerous as to be incapable of pursuing the objects of its passions, by means which reason prescribes; it is against the enterprising ambition of this department that the people ought to indulge all their jealousy and exhaust all their precautions.

The legislative department derives a superiority in our governments from other circumstances. Its constitutional powers being at once more extensive, and less susceptible of precise limits, it can, with the greater facility, mask, under complicated and indirect measures, the encroachments which it makes on the coördinate departments. It is not unfrequently a question of real nicety in legislative bodies, whether the operation of a particular measure will, or will not, extend beyond the legislative sphere. On the other side, the executive power being restrained within a narrower compass, and being more simple in its nature, and the judiciary being described by landmarks still less uncertain, projects of usurpation by either of these departments would immediately betray and defeat themselves. Nor is this all: as the legislative department alone has access to the pockets of the people, and has in some constitutions full discretion, and in all a prevailing influence, over the pecuniary rewards of those who fill the other departments, a dependence is thus created in the latter, which gives still greater facility to encroachments of the former.

I have appealed to our own experience for the truth of what I advance on this subject. Were it necessary to verify this experience by particular proofs, they might be multiplied without end. I might find a witness in every citizen who has shared in, or been attentive to, the course of public administrations. I might collect vouchers in abundance from the records and archives of every State in the Union. But as a more concise, and at the same time equally satisfactory, evidence, I will refer to the example of two States, attested by two unexceptionable authorities.

The first example is that of Virginia, a State which, as we have seen, has expressly declared in its constitution, that the three great departments ought not to be intermixed. The authority in support of it is Mr. Jefferson, who, besides his other advantages for remarking the operation of the government, was himself the chief magistrate of it. In order to convey fully the ideas with which his experience had impressed him on this subject, it will be necessary to quote a passage of some length from his very interesting "Notes on the State of Virginia," p. 195. "All the powers of government, legislative, executive, and judiciary, result to the legislative body. The concentrating these in the same hands, is precisely the definition of despotic government. It will be no alleviation, that these powers will be exercised by a plurality of hands, and not by a single one. One hundred and seventy-three despots would surely be as oppressive as one. Let those who doubt it, turn their eyes on the republic of Venice. As little will it avail us, that they are chosen by ourselves. An *elective despotism* was not the government we fought for; but one which should not only be founded on free principles, but in which the powers of government should be so divided and balanced among several bodies of magistracy, as that no one could transcend their legal limits, without being effectually checked and restrained by the others. For this reason, that convention which passed the ordinance of government, laid its foundation on this basis, that the legislative, executive, and judiciary departments should be separate and distinct, so that no person should exercise the powers of more than one of them at the same time. *But no barrier was provided between these several powers.* The judiciary and the executive members were left dependent on the legislative for their subsistence in office, and some of them for their continuance in it. If, therefore, the legislature assumes executive and judiciary powers, no opposition is likely to be made; nor, if made, can be effectual; because in that case they may put their proceedings into the form of acts of Assembly, which will render them obligatory on the other branches. They have accordingly, *in many* instances, *decided rights* which should have been left to *judiciary controversy,* and *the direction of the executive, during the whole time of their session, is becoming habitual and familiar.*"

The other State which I shall take for an example is Pennsylvania; and the other authority, the Council of Censors, which assembled in the years 1783 and 1784. A part of the duty of this body, as marked out by the constitution, was "to inquire whether the constitution had been preserved inviolate in every part; and whether the legislative and executive branches of government had performed their duty as guardians of the people, or assumed to themselves, or exercised, other or greater powers than they are entitled to by the constitution." In the execution of this trust, the council were necessarily led to a comparison of both the legislative and executive proceedings, with the constitutional powers of these departments; and from the facts enumerated, and to the truth of most of which both sides in the council subscribed, it appears that the constitution had been flagrantly violated by the legislature in a variety of important instances.

A great number of laws had been passed, violating, without any apparent necessity, the rule requiring that all bills of a public nature shall be previously printed for the consideration of the people; although this is one of the precautions chiefly relied on by the constitution against improper acts of the legislature.

The constitutional trial by jury had been violated, and powers assumed which had not been delegated by the constitution.

Executive powers had been usurped.

The salaries of the judges, which the constitution expressly requires to be fixed, had been occasionally varied; and cases belonging to the judiciary department frequently drawn within legislative cognizance and determination.

Those who wish to see the several particulars falling under each of these heads, may consult the journals of the council, which are in print. Some of them, it will be found, may be imputable to peculiar circumstances connected with the war; but the greater part of them may be considered as the spontaneous shoots of an ill-constituted government.

It appears, also, that the executive department had not been innocent of frequent breaches of the constitution. There are three observations, however, which ought to be made on this head: *first,* a great proportion of the instances were either immediately produced by the necessities of the war, or recommended by Congress or the commander-in-chief; *secondly,* in most of the other instances, they conformed either to the declared or the known sentiments of the legislative department; *thirdly,* the executive department of Pennsylvania is distinguished from that of the other States by the number of members composing it. In this respect, it has as much affinity to a legislative assembly as to an executive council. And being at once exempt from the restraint of an individual responsibility for the acts of the body, and deriving confidence from mutual example and joint influence, unauthorized measures would, of course, be more freely hazarded, than where the executive department is administered by a single hand, or by a few hands.

The conclusion which I am warranted in drawing from these observations is, that a mere demarcation on parchment of the constitutional limits of the several departments, is not a sufficient guard against those encroachments which lead to a tyrannical concentration of all the powers of government in the same hands. PUBLIUS

FEDERALIST NO. 51

By Alexander Hamilton or James Madison

This paper was originally published in the New York Packet *on February 8, 1788.*

To what expedient, then, shall we finally resort, for maintaining in practice the necessary partition of power among the several departments, as laid down in the Constitution? The only answer that can be given is, that as all these exterior provisions are found to be inadequate, the defect must be supplied, by so contriving the interior structure of the government as that its several constituent parts may, by their mutual relations, be the means of keeping each other in their proper places. Without presuming to undertake a full development of this important idea, I will hazard a few general observations, which may perhaps place it in a clearer light, and enable us to form a more correct judgment of the principles and structure of the government planned by the convention.

In order to lay a due foundation for that separate and distinct exercise of the different powers of government, which to a certain extent is admitted on all hands to be essential to the preservation of liberty, it is evident that each department should have a will of its own; and consequently should be so constituted that the members of each should have as little agency as possible in the appointment of the members of the others. Were this principle rigorously adhered to, it would require that all the appointments for the supreme executive, legislative, and judiciary magistracies should be drawn from the same fountain of authority, the people, through channels having no communication whatever with one another. Perhaps such a plan of constructing the several departments would be less difficult in practice than it may in contemplation appear. Some difficulties, however, and some additional expense would attend the execution of it. Some deviations, therefore, from the principle must be admitted. In the constitution of the judiciary department in particular, it might be inexpedient to insist rigorously on the principle: first, because peculiar qualifications being essential in the members, the primary consideration ought to be to select that mode of choice which best secures these qualifications; secondly, because the permanent tenure by which the appointments are held in that department, must soon destroy all sense of dependence on the authority conferring them.

It is equally evident, that the members of each department should be as little dependent as possible on those of the others, for the emoluments annexed to their offices. Were the executive magistrate, or the judges, not independent of the legislature in this particular, their independence in every other would be merely nominal.

But the great security against a gradual concentration of the several powers in the same department, consists in giving to those who administer each department the necessary constitutional means and personal motives to resist encroachments of the others. The provision for defence must in this, as in all other cases, be made commensurate to the danger of attack. Ambition must be made to counteract ambition. The interest of the man must be connected with the constitutional rights of the place. It may be a reflection on human nature, that such devices should be necessary to control the abuses of government. But what is government itself, but the greatest of all reflections on human nature? If men were angels, no government would be necessary. If angels were to govern men, neither external nor internal controls on government would be necessary. In framing a government which is to be administered by men over men, the great difficulty lies in this: you must first enable the government to control the governed; and in the next place oblige it to control itself. A dependence on the people is, no doubt, the primary control on the government; but experience has taught mankind the necessity of auxiliary precautions.

This policy of supplying, by opposite and rival interests, the defect of better motives, might be traced through the whole system of human affairs, private as well as public. We see it particularly displayed in all the subordinate distributions of power, where the constant aim is to divide and arrange the several offices in such a manner as that each may be a check on the other—that the private interest of every individual may be a sentinel over the public rights. These inventions of prudence cannot be less requisite in the distribution of the supreme powers of the State.

But it is not possible to give to each department an equal power of self-defence. In republican government, the legislative authority necessarily predominates. The remedy for this inconveniency is to divide the legislature into different branches; and to render them, by different modes of election and different principles of action, as little connected with each other as the nature of their common functions and their common dependence on the society will admit. It may even be necessary to guard against dangerous encroachments by still further precautions. As the weight of the legislative authority requires that it should be thus divided, the weakness of the executive may require, on the other hand, that it should be fortified. An absolute negative on the legislature appears, at first view, to be the natural defence with which the executive magistrate should be armed. But perhaps it would be neither altogether safe nor alone sufficient. On ordinary occasions it might not be exerted with the requisite firmness, and on extraordinary occasions it might be perfidiously abused. May not this defect of an absolute negative be supplied by some qualified connection between this weaker department and the weaker branch of the stronger department, by which the latter may be led to support the constitutional rights of the former, without being too much detached from the rights of its own department?

If the principles on which these observations are founded be just, as I persuade myself they are, and they be applied as a criterion to the several State constitutions, and to the federal Constitution, it will be found that if the latter does not perfectly correspond with them, the former are infinitely less able to bear such a test.

There are, moreover, two considerations particularly applicable to the federal system of America, which place that system in a very interesting point of view.

First. In a single republic, all the power surrendered by the people is submitted to the administration of a single government; and the usurpations are guarded against by a division of the government into distinct and separate departments. In the compound republic of America, the power surrendered by the people is first divided between two distinct governments, and then the portion allotted to each subdivided among distinct and separate departments. Hence a double security arises to the rights of the people. The different governments will control each other, at the same time that each will be controlled by itself.

Second. It is of great importance in a republic not only to guard the society against the oppression of its rulers, but to guard one part of the society against the injustice of the other part. Different interests necessarily exist in different classes of citizens. If a majority be united by a common interest, the rights of the minority will be insecure. There are but two methods of providing against this evil: the one by creating a will in the community independent of the majority—that is, of the society itself; the other, by comprehending in the society so many separate descriptions of citizens as will render an unjust combination of a majority of the whole very improbable, if not impracticable. The first method prevails in all governments possessing an hereditary or self-appointed authority. This, at best, is but a precarious security; because a power independent of the society may as well espouse the unjust views of the major, as the rightful interests of the minor party, and may possibly be turned against both parties. The second method will be exemplified in the federal republic of the United States. Whilst all authority in it will be derived from and dependent on the society, the society itself will be broken into so many parts, interests and classes of citizens, that the rights of individuals, or of the minority, will be in little danger from interested combinations of the majority. In a free government the security for civil rights must be the same as that for religious rights. It consists in the one case in the multiplicity of interests, and in the other in the multiplicity of sects. The degree of security in both cases will depend on the number of interests and sects; and this may be presumed to depend on the extent of country and number of people comprehended under the same government. This view of the subject must particularly recommend a proper federal system to all the sincere and considerate friends of republican government, since it shows that in exact proportion as the territory of the Union may be formed into more circumscribed Confederacies, or States, oppressive combinations of a majority will be facilitated; the best security, under the republican forms, for the rights of every class of citizens, will be diminished; and consequently the stability and independence of some member of the government, the only other security, must be proportionally increased. Justice is the end of government. It is the end of civil society. It ever has been and ever will be pursued until it be obtained, or until liberty be lost in the pursuit. In a society under the forms of which the stronger faction can readily unite and oppress the weaker, anarchy may as truly be said to reign as in a state of nature, where the weaker individual is not secured against the violence of the stronger; and as, in the latter state, even the stronger individuals are prompted, by the uncertainty of their condition, to submit to a government which may protect the weak as well as themselves; so, in the former state, will the more powerful factions or parties be gradually induced, by a like motive, to wish for a government which will protect all parties, the weaker as well as the more powerful. It can be little doubted that if the State of Rhode Island was separated from the Confederacy and left to itself, the insecurity of rights under the popular form of government within such narrow limits would be displayed by such reiterated oppressions of factious majorities that some power altogether independent of the people would soon be called for by the voice of the very factions whose misrule had proved the necessity of it. In the extended republic of the United States, and among the great variety of interests, parties, and sects which it embraces, a coalition of a majority of the whole society could seldom take place on any other principles than those of justice and the general good; whilst there being thus less danger to a minor from the will of a major party, there must be less pretext, also, to provide for the security of the former, by introducing into the government a will not dependent on the latter, or, in other words, a will independent of the society itself. It is no less certain than it is important, notwithstanding the contrary opinions which have been entertained, that the larger the society, provided it lie within a practical sphere, the more duly capable it will be of self-government. And happily for the *republican cause,* the practicable sphere may be carried to a very great extent, by a judicious modification and mixture of the *federal principle.* PUBLIUS

McCULLOCH v. MARYLAND *

The Supreme Court of the United States has been the most authoritative and articulate voice in recording the changes in American constitutional practice and in elaborating and explaining the provisions of its foundation

* 4 Wheaton (U.S.) 316 (1819).

document. In this early and extremely important case the nature of the federal relationship is expounded.

Marshall, Chief Justice, delivered the opinion of the Court, saying in part:

In the case now to be determined, the defendant, a sovereign state, denies the obligation of a law enacted by the legislature of the Union, and the plaintiff, on his part, contests the validity of an act which has been passed by the legislature of that state. The constitution of our country, in its most interesting and vital parts, is to be considered; the conflicting powers of the government of the Union and of its members, as marked in that constitution, are to be discussed; and an opinion given, which may essentially influence the great operations of the government. . . .

The first question made in the cause is, has Congress power to incorporate a bank?

It has been truly said that this can scarcely be considered as an open question. . . . The principle now contested was introduced at a very early period of our history, has been recognized by many successive legislatures, and has been acted upon by the judicial department, in cases of peculiar delicacy, as a law of undoubted obligation. . . .

In discussing this question, the counsel for the state of Maryland have deemed it of some importance, in the construction of the constitution, to consider that instrument not as emanating from the people, but as the act of sovereign and independent states. The powers of the general government, it has been said, are delegated by the states, who alone are truly sovereign; and must be exercised in subordination to the states, who alone possess supreme dominion.

It would be difficult to sustain this proposition. The convention which framed the constitution was indeed elected by the state legislatures. But the instrument, when it came from their hands, was a mere proposal, without obligation, or pretensions to it. It was reported to the then existing Congress of the United States, with a request that it might "be submitted to a convention of delegates, chosen in each state by the people thereof, under the recommendation of its legislature, for their assent and ratification." This mode of proceeding was adopted; and by the convention, by Congress, and by the state legislatures, the instrument was submitted to the people. They acted upon it in the only manner they can act safely, effectively, and wisely, on such a subject, by assembling in convention. It is true, they assembled in their several states—and where else should they have assembled? No political dreamer was ever wild enough to think of breaking down the lines which separate the states, and of compounding the American people into one common mass. Of consequence, when they act, they act in their states. But the measures they adopt do not, on that account, cease to be the measures of the people themselves, or become the measures of the state governments.

From these conventions the constitution derives its whole authority. . . . The constitution, when thus adopted, was of complete obligation, and bound the state sovereignties. . . .

The government of the Union, then . . . is, emphatically, and truly, a government of the people. In form and in substance it emanates from them. Its powers are granted by them, and are to be exercised directly on them, and for their benefit.

The government is acknowledged by all to be one of enumerated powers. . . . But the question respecting the extent of the powers actually granted, is perpetually arising, and will probably continue to arise, as long as our system shall exist.

In discussing these questions, the conflicting powers of the general and state governments must be brought into view, and the supremacy of their respective laws, when they are in opposition, must be settled.

If any one proposition could command the universal assent of mankind, we might expect it would be this—that the government of the Union, though limited in its powers, is supreme within its sphere of action. This would seem to result necessarily from its nature. It is the government of all; its powers are delegated by all; it represents all, and acts for all. . . . But this question is not left to mere reason; the people have, in express terms, decided it by saying, "this constitution, and the laws of the United States, which shall be made in pursuance thereof," "shall be the supreme law of the land," and by requiring that the members of the state legislatures, and the officers of the executive and judicial departments of the states shall take the oath of fidelity to it.

The government of the United States, then, though limited in its powers, is supreme; and its laws, when made in pursuance of the constitution, form the supreme law of the land, "anything in the constitution or laws, of any state to the contrary notwithstanding."

Among the enumerated powers, we do not find that of establishing a bank or creating a corporation. But there is no phrase in the instrument which, like the articles of confederation, excludes incidental or implied powers; and which requires that everything granted shall be expressly and minutely described. Even the 10th amendment, which was framed for the purpose of quieting the excessive jealousies which had been excited, omits the word "expressly," and declares only that the powers "not delegated to the United States, nor prohibited to the states, are reserved to the states or to the people;" thus leaving the question, whether the particular power which may become the subject of contest has been delegated to the one government, or prohibited to the other, to depend on a fair construction of the whole instrument. The men who drew and adopted this amendment had experienced the embarrassments resulting from the insertion of this word in the articles of confederation, and probably omitted it to avoid those embarrassments. A constitution, to contain an accurate detail of all the subdivisions of which its great powers will admit, and of all the means by which they may be carried into execution, would partake of the prolixity of a legal code, and could scarcely be embraced by the human mind. It would probably never be understood by the public. Its nature, therefore, requires, that only its great outlines should be marked, its important objects designated, and the minor ingredients which compose those objects be deduced from the nature of the objects themselves. That this idea was entertained by the framers of the American constitution, is not only to be inferred from the nature of the instrument, but from the language. Why else were some of the limitations, found in the ninth section of the 1st article, introduced? It is also, in some degree, warranted by their having omitted to use any restrictive term which might prevent its receiving a fair and just interpretation. In considering this question, then, we must never forget that it is a constitution we are expounding.

Although, among the enumerated powers of government, we do not find the word "bank" or "incorporation," we find the great powers to lay and collect taxes; to borrow money; to regulate commerce; to declare and conduct a war; and to raise and support armies and navies. The sword and the purse, all the external relations, and no inconsiderable portion of the industry of the nation, are entrusted to its government. It can never be pretended that these vast powers draw after them others of inferior importance, merely because they are inferior. Such an idea can never be advanced. But it may with great reason be contended, that a government, entrusted with such ample powers, on the due execution of which the happiness and prosperity of the nation so vitally depends, must also be entrusted with ample means for their execution. The power being given, it is the interest of the nation to facilitate its execution. It can never be their interest, and cannot be presumed to have been their intention, to clog and embarrass its execution by withholding the most appropriate means. . . .

The government which has a right to do an act, and has imposed on it the duty of performing that act, must, according to the dictates of reason, be allowed to select the means. . . .

The power of creating a corporation, though appertaining to sovereignty, is not, like the power of making war, or levying taxes, or of regulating commerce, a great substantive and independent power, which cannot be implied as incidental to other powers, or used as a means of executing them. It is never the end for which other powers are exercised, but a means by which other objects are accomplished. No contributions are made to charity for the sake of an incorporation, but a corporation is created to administer the charity; no seminary of learning is instituted in order to be incorporated, but the corporate character is conferred to subserve the purposes of education. . . . The power of creating a corporation is never used for its own sake, but for the purpose of effecting something else. No sufficient reason is, therefore, perceived, why it may not pass as incidental to those powers which are expressly given, if it be a direct mode of executing them.

But the constitution of the United States has not left the right of Congress to employ the necessary means for the execution of the powers conferred on the government to general reasoning. To its enumeration of powers is added that of making "all laws which shall be necessary and proper, for carrying into execution the foregoing powers, and all other powers vested by this constitution, in the government of the United States, or in any department thereof."

The counsel for the State of Maryland have urged various arguments, to prove that this clause, though in terms a grant of power, is not so in effect; but is really restrictive of the general right, which might otherwise be implied, of selecting means for executing the enumerated powers.

In support of this proposition, they have found it necessary to contend, that this clause was inserted for the purpose of conferring on Congress the power of making laws. . . .

But could this be the object for which it was inserted? A government is created by the people, having legislative, executive, and judicial powers. Its legislative powers are vested in a Congress, which is to consist of a senate and house of representatives. Each house may determine the rule of its proceedings; and it is declared that every bill which shall have passed both houses, shall, before it becomes a law, be presented to the President of the United States. The 7th section describes the course of proceedings, by which a bill shall become a law; and, then, the 8th section enumerates the powers of Congress. Could it be necessary to say that a legislature should exercise legislative powers in the shape of legislation? . . .

But the argument on which most reliance is placed, is drawn from the peculiar language of this clause. Congress is not empowered by it to make all laws, which may have relation to the powers conferred on the government, but such only as may be "necessary and proper" for carrying them into execution. The word "necessary" is considered as controlling the whole sentence, and as limiting the right to pass laws for the execution of the granted powers, to such as are indispensable, and without which the power would be nugatory. That it excludes the choice of means, and leaves to Congress, in each case, that only which is most direct and simple.

Is it true that this is the sense in which the word "necessary" is always used? Does it always import an absolute physical necessity, so strong that one thing, to which another may be termed necessary, cannot exist without that other? We think it does not. If reference be had to its use, in the common affairs of the world, or in approved authors, we find that it frequently imports no more than that one thing is convenient, or useful, or essential to another. To employ the means necessary to an end, is generally understood as employing any means calculated to produce the end, and not as being confined to those single means, without which the end would be entirely unattainable. Such is the character of human language, that no word conveys to the mind, in all situations, one single definite idea; and nothing is more common than to use words in a figurative sense. . . . The word "necessary" is of this description. It has not a fixed character peculiar to itself. It admits of all degrees of comparison; and is often connected with other words, which increase or diminish the impression the mind receives of the urgency it imports. A thing may be necessary, very necessary, absolutely or indispensably necessary. To no mind would the same idea be conveyed by these several phrases. This comment on the word is well illustrated by the passage cited at the bar, from the 10th section of the 1st article of the constitution. It is, we think, impossible to compare the sentence which prohibits a state from laying "imposts or duties on imports or exports, except what may be absolutely necessary for executing its inspection laws," with that which authorizes Congress "to make all laws which shall be necessary and proper for carrying into execution" the powers of the general government, without feeling a conviction that the convention understood itself to change materially the meaning of the word "necessary," by prefixing the word "absolutely." This word, then, like others, is used in various senses; and, in its construction, the subject, the context, the intention of the person using them, are all to be taken into view.

Let this be done in the case under consideration. The subject is the execution of those great powers on which the welfare of a nation essentially depends. It must have been the intention of those who gave these powers, to insure, as far as human prudence could insure, their beneficial execution. This could not be done by confiding the choice of means to such narrow limits as not to leave it in the power of Congress to adopt any which might be appropriate, and which were conducive to the end. This provision is made in a constitution intended to endure for ages to come, and, consequently, to be adapted to the various crises of human affairs. To have prescribed the means by which government should, in all future time, execute its powers, would have been to change, entirely, the character of the instrument, and give it the properties of a legal code. It would have been an unwise attempt to provide, by immutable rules, for exigencies which, if foreseen at all, must have been seen dimly, and which can be best provided for as they occur. To have declared that the best means shall not be used, but those alone without which the power given would be nugatory, would have been to deprive the legislature of the capacity to avail itself of experience, to exercise its reason, and to accommodate its legislation to circumstances. . . .

But the argument which most conclusively demonstrates the error of the construction contended for by the counsel for the state of Maryland, is founded on the intention of the convention, as manifested in the whole clause. To waste time and argument in proving that without it Congress might carry its powers into execution, would be not much less idle, than to hold a lighted taper to the sun. As little can it be required to prove, that in the absence of this clause, Congress would have some choice of means. That it might employ those which, in its judgment, would most advantageously effect the object to be accomplished. That any means adapted to the end, any means which tended directly to the execution of the constitutional powers to the government, were in themselves constitutional. This clause, as construed by the state of Maryland, would abridge, and almost annihilate this useful and necessary right of the legislature to select its means. That this could not be intended, is, we should think, had it not been already controverted, too apparent for controversy. We think so for the following reasons:

1st. The clause is placed among the powers of Congress, not among the limitations on those powers.

2nd. Its terms purport to enlarge, not to diminish the powers vested in the government. It purports to be an additional power, not a restriction on those already granted. No reason has been, or can be assigned for thus concealing an intention to narrow the discretion of the national legislature under words which purport to enlarge it. The framers of the constitution wished its adoption, and well knew that it would be endangered by its strength, not by its weakness. . . . If, then, their intention had been, by this clause, to restrain the free use of means which might otherwise have been implied, that intention would have been inserted in another place, and would have been expressed in terms resembling these. "In carrying into execution the foregoing powers, and all others," etc., "no laws shall be passed but such as are necessary and proper." Had the intention been to make this clause restrictive, it would unquestionably have been so in form as well as in effect.

The result of the most careful and attentive consideration bestowed upon this clause is, that if it does not enlarge, it cannot be construed to restrain the powers of Congress, or to impair the right of the legislature to exercise its best judgment in the selection of measures to carry into execution the constitutional powers of the government. If no other motive for its insertion can be suggested, a sufficient one is found in the desire to remove all doubts respecting the right to legislate on that vast mass of incidental powers which must be involved in the constitution, if that instrument be not a splendid bauble.

We admit, as all must admit, that the powers of the government are limited, and that its limits are not to be transcended. But we think the sound construction of the constitution must allow to the national legislature that discretion, with respect to the means by which the powers it confers are to be carried into execution, which will enable that body to perform the high duties assigned to it, in the manner most beneficial to the people. Let the end be legitimate, let it be within the scope of the constitution, and all means which are appropriate, which are plainly adapted to that end, which are not prohibited, but consist with the letter and spirit of the constitution, are constitutional . . .

The power to "make all needful rules and regulations respecting the territory or other property belonging to the United States," [Sec. 3, Art. 4] is not more comprehensive, than the power "to make all laws which shall be necessary and proper for carrying into execution" the powers of the government. Yet all admit the constitutionality of a territorial government, which is a corporate body.

If a corporation may be employed indiscriminately with other means to carry into execution the powers of the government, no particular reason can be assigned for excluding the use of a bank, if required for its fiscal operations. To use one, must be within the discretion of Congress, if it be an appropriate mode of executing the powers of government. That it is a convenient, a useful, and essential instrument in the prosecution of its fiscal operations, is not now a subject of controversy. All those who have been concerned in the administration of our finances, have concurred in representing the importance and necessity . . .

But, were its necessity less apparent, none can deny its being an appropriate measure; and if it is, the degree of its necessity, as has been very justly observed, is to be discussed in another place. Should Congress, in the execution of its powers, adopt measures which are prohibited by the constitution; or should Congress, under the pretext of executing its powers, pass laws for the accomplishment of objects not entrusted to the government, it would become the painful duty of this tribunal, should a case requiring such a decision come before it, to say that such an act was not the law of the land. But where the law is not prohibited, and is really calculated to effect any of the objects entrusted to the government, to undertake here to inquire into the degree of its necessity, would be to pass the line which circumscribes the judicial department, and to tread on legislative ground. . . .

It being the opinion of the court that the act incorporating the bank is constitutional, and that the power of establishing a branch in the state of Maryland might be properly exercised by the bank itself, we proceed to inquire:

2. Whether the state of Maryland may, without violating the constitution, tax that branch?

That the power of taxation is one of vital importance; that it is retained by the states; that it is not abridged by the grant of a similar power to the government of the Union; that it is to be concurrently exercised by the two governments: are truths which have never been denied. But, such is the paramount character of the constitution that its capacity to withdraw any subject from the action of even this power, is admitted. The states are expressly forbidden to lay any duties on imports or exports, except what may be absolutely necessary for executing their inspection laws. If the obligation of this prohibition must be conceded—if it may restrain a state from the exercise of its taxing power on imports and exports—the same paramount character would seem to restrain, as it certainly may restrain, a state from such other exercise of this power, as is in its nature incompatible with, and repugnant to, the constitutional laws of the Union. A law, absolutely repugnant to another, as entirely repeals that other as if express terms of repeal were used.

On this ground the counsel for the bank place its claim to be exempted from the power of a state to tax its operations. There is no express provision for the case, but the claim has been sustained on a principle which so entirely pervades the constitution, is so intermixed with the materials which compose it, so interwoven with its web, so blended with its texture, as to be incapable of being separated from it without rendering it into shreds.

This great principle is, that the constitution and the laws made in pursuance thereof are supreme; that they control the constitution and laws of the respective states, and cannot be controlled by them. From this, which may be almost termed an axiom, other propositions are deduced as corollaries, on the truth or error of which, and on their application to this case, the cause has been supposed to depend. These are, 1st, that a power to create implies a power to preserve. 2d. That a power to destroy, if wielded by a different hand, is hostile to, and incompatible with these powers to create and to preserve. 3d. That where this repugnancy exists, that authority which is supreme must control, not yield to that over which it is supreme . . .

All subjects over which the sovereign power of a state extends, are objects of taxation; but those over which it does not extend, are, upon the soundest principles, exempt from taxation . . .

The sovereignty of a state extends to everything which exists by its own authority, or is introduced by its permission; but does it extend to those means which are employed by Congress to carry into execution powers conferred on that body by the people of the United States? We think it demonstrable that it does not. Those powers are not given by the people of a single state. They are given by the people of the United States, to a government whose laws, made in pursuance of the constitution, are declared to be supreme. Consequently, the people of a single state cannot confer a sovereignty which will extend over them . . .

That the power to tax involves the power to destroy; that the power to destroy may defeat and render useless the power to create; that there is a plain repugnance, in conferring on one government a power to control the constitutional measures of another, which other, with respect to those very measures, is declared to be supreme over that which exerts the control, are propositions not to be denied. But all inconsistencies are to be reconciled by the magic of the word *confidence*. Taxation, it is said, does not necessarily and unavoidably destroy. To carry it to the excess of destruction would be an abuse, to presume which, would banish that confidence which is essential to all government.

But is this a case of confidence? Would the people of any one state trust those of another with a power to control the most insignificant operations of their state government? We know they would not. Why, then, should we suppose that the people of any one state should be willing to trust those of another with a power to control the operations of a government to which they have confided the most important and most valuable interests? In the legislature of the Union alone, are all represented. The legislature of the Union alone, therefore, can be trusted by the people with the power of controlling measures which concern all, in the confidence that it will not be abused. This, then, is not a case of confidence, and we must consider it as it really is.

If we apply the principle for which the state of Maryland contends, to the constitution generally, we shall find it capable of changing totally this character of that instrument. . . . The American people have declared their constitution, and the laws made in pursuance thereof, to be supreme; but this principle would transfer the supremacy, in fact, to the states.

If the states may tax one instrument, employed by the government in the execution of its powers, they may tax any and every other instrument. They may tax the mail; they may tax the mint; they may tax patent-rights; they may tax the papers of the custom-house; they may tax judicial process; they may tax all the means employed by the government, to an excess which would defeat all the ends of government. This was not intended by the American people. They did not design to make their government dependent on the states . . .

It has also been insisted, that, as the power of taxation in the general and state governments is acknowledged to be concurrent, every argument which would sustain the right of the general government to tax banks chartered by the states, will equally sustain the right of the states to tax banks chartered by the general government.

But the two cases are not on the same reason. The people of all the states have created the general government, and have conferred upon it the general power of taxation. The people of all the states, and the states themselves, are represented in Congress, and, by their representatives, exercise this power. When they tax the chartered institutions of the states, they tax their constituents; and these taxes must be uniform. But, when a state taxes the operations of the government of the United States, it acts upon institutions created, not by their own constituents, but by people over whom they claim no control. It acts upon the measures of a government created by others as well as themselves, for the benefit of others in common with themselves. . . .

The court has bestowed on this subject its most deliberate consideration. The result is a conviction that the states have no power, by taxation or otherwise, to retard, impede, burden, or in any manner control the operations of the constitutional laws enacted by Congress to carry into execution the powers vested in the general government. This is, we think, the unavoidable consequence of that supremacy which the constitution has declared.

We are unanimously of opinion that the law passed by the legislature of Maryland, imposing a tax on the Bank of the United States, is unconstitutional and void.

This opinion does not deprive the states of any resources which they originally possessed. It does not extend to a tax paid by the real property of the bank, in common with the other real property within the state, nor to a tax imposed on the interest which the citizens of Maryland may hold in this institution, in common with other property of the same description, throughout the state. But this is a tax on the operations of the bank, and is, consequently, a tax on the operation of an instrument employed by the government of the Union to carry its powers into execution. Such a tax must be unconstitutional.

POPULAR SOVEREIGNTY IN AMERICA*

by Alexis de Tocqueville

The Founders of the American Republic deliberately incorporated in its Constitution principles of federalism, separation of powers, constitutionalism, etc. They did not similarly enshrine democracy. Yet, that frail plant —so rare and exotic at the time—soon took root in the

* From *Democracy in America* (Trans. by Henry Reeves), Geo. Dearborn & Co., New York, 1838, pp. 35-39. A few minor textual changes have been made.

rich soil of the New World and by the second quarter of the 19th century was in full flower. Since then it has been regarded universally as a fundamental principle of our government.

Because the Founders did not create a democracy, The Federalist *did not defend that concept and the Supreme Court has no Constitutional guarantee of democracy on which it can expound. But about the time democracy had become fully accepted in the United States, a young French nobleman, Alexis de Tocqueville, visited these shores and observed the phenomenon with rare perception. By explaining our system to his countrymen he explained it to ourselves so cogently and lucidly that his study has become a classic. No American has matched it despite the passage of more than 125 years.*

The following selection is only one brief passage from a detailed, two-volume work, but it summarizes de Tocqueville's underlying theme.

America exhibits in her social state a most extraordinary phenomenon. Men are there seen on a greater equality in point of fortune and intellect, or, in other words, more equal in their strength, than in any other country of the world, or, in any age of which history has preserved the remembrance. . . .

The political consequences of such a social condition as this are easily deducible.

It is impossible to believe that equality will not eventually find its way into the political world as it does everywhere else. To conceive of men remaining forever unequal upon one single point, yet equal on all others, is impossible; they must come in the end to be equal upon all.

Now I know of only two methods of establishing equality in the political world: every citizen must be put in possession of his rights, or rights must be granted to no one. For nations which are arrived at the same stage of social existence as the Anglo-Americans, it is therefore very difficult to discover a medium between the sovereignty of all and the absolute power of one man: and it would be vain to deny that the social condition which I have been describing is equally liable to each of these consequences.

There is, in fact, a manly and lawful passion for equality which excites men to wish all to be powerful and honored. This passion tends to elevate the humble to the rank of the great; but there exists also in the human heart a depraved taste for equality, which impels the weak to attempt to lower the powerful to their own level, and reduces men to prefer equality in slavery to inequality with freedom. Not that those nations whose social condition is democratic naturally despise liberty; on the contrary, they have an instinctive love of it. But liberty is not the chief and constant object of their desires; equality is their idol: they make rapid and sudden efforts to obtain liberty, and if they miss their aim, resign themselves to their disappointment; but nothing can satisfy them except equality, and rather than lose it they resolve to perish.

On the other hand, in a state where the citizens are nearly equal, it becomes difficult for them to preserve their independence against the aggressions of power. No one among them being strong enough to engage singly in the struggle with advantage, nothing but a general combination can protect their liberty: and such a union is not always to be found.

From the same social position, then, nations may derive one or the other of two great political results; these results are extremely different from each other, but they may both proceed from the same cause.

The Anglo-Americans are the first who, having been exposed to this formidable alternative, have been happy enough to escape the dominion of absolute power. They have been allowed by their circumstances, their origin, their intelligence, and especially by their moral feeling, to establish and maintain the sovereignty of the people.

Whenever the political laws of the United States are to be discussed, it is with the doctrine of the sovereignty of the people that we must begin.

The principle of the sovereignty of the people, which is to be found, more or less, at the bottom of almost all human institutions, generally remains concealed from view. It is obeyed without being recognised, or if for a moment it be brought to light, it is hastily cast back into the gloom of the sanctuary.

'The will of the nation' is one of those expressions which have been most profusely abused by the wily and the despotic of every age. To the eyes of some it has been represented by the venal suffrages of a few of the satellites of power; to others, by the votes of a timid or an interested minority; and some have even discovered it in the silence of a people, on the supposition that the fact of submission established the right of command.

In America, the principle of the sovereignty of the people is neither barren nor concealed, as it is with some other nations; it is recognized by the customs and proclaimed by the laws; it spreads freely, and arrives without impediment at its most remote consequences. If there be a country in the world where the doctrine of the sovereignty of the people can be fairly appreciated, where it can be studied in its application to the affairs of society, and where its dangers and its advantages may be foreseen, that country is assuredly America.

I have already observed that, from their origin, the sovereignty of the people was the fundamental principle of the greater number of British colonies in America. However, it was far from exercising then as much influence on the government of society as it now does. Two obstacles, the one external, the other internal, checked its invasive progress.

It could not ostensibly disclose itself in the laws of colonies which were still constrained to obey the mother-country; it was therefore obliged to spread secretly, and to gain ground in the provincial assemblies, and especially in the townships.

American society was not yet prepared to adopt it with all its consequences. The intelligence of New England, and the wealth of the country to the south of the Hudson . . . long exercised a sort of aristocratic influence which tended to limit the exercise of social authority within the hands of a few. The public functionaries were not universally elected, and the citizens were not all of them electors. The electoral franchise was everywhere placed within certain limits, and made dependent on a certain qualification, which was exceedingly low in the North and more considerable in the South.

The American revolution broke out, and the doctrine

of the sovereignty of the people, which had been nurtured in the townships, took possession of the State: every class was enlisted in its cause; battles were fought, and victories obtained for it; until it became the law of laws.

A scarcely less rapid change was effected in the interior of society, where the law of descent completed the abolition of local influences.

At the very time when this consequence of the laws and of the revolution became apparent to every eye, victory was irrevocably pronounced in favor of the democratic cause. All power was, in fact, in its hands, and resistance was no longer possible. The higher orders submitted without a murmur and without a struggle to an evil which was thenceforth inevitable. The ordinary fate of falling powers awaited them; each of their several members followed his own interest; and as it was impossible to wring the power from the hands of a people which they did not detest sufficiently to brave, their own aim was to secure its good will at any price. The most democratic laws were consequently voted by the very men whose interests they impaired: and thus, although the higher classes did not excite the passions of the people against their order, they accelerated the triumph of the new state of things; so that, by a singular change, the democratic impulse was found to be most irresistible in the very States where the aristocracy had the firmest hold.

The State of Maryland, which had been founded by men of rank, was the first to proclaim universal suffrage, and to introduce the most democratic forms into the conduct of its government.

When a nation modifies the elective qualification, it may easily be foreseen that sooner or later that qualification will be entirely abolished. There is no more invariable rule in the history of society: the further electoral rights are extended, the more is felt the need of extending them; for after each concession the strength of the democracy increases, and its demands increase with its strength. The ambition of those who are below the appointed rate is irritated in exact proportion to the great number of those who are above it. The exception at last becomes the rule, concession follows concession, and no stop can be made short of universal suffrage.

At the present day the principle of the sovereignty of the people has acquired, in the United States, all the practical development which the imagination can conceive. It is unencumbered by those fictions which have been thrown over it in other countries, and it appears in every possible form according to the exigency of the occasion. Sometimes the laws are made by the people in a body, as at Athens; and sometimes its representatives, chosen by universal suffrage, transact business in its name, and almost under its immediate control.

In some countries a power exists which, though it is in a degree foreign to the social body, directs it, and forces it to pursue a certain track. In others the ruling force is divided, being partly within and partly without the ranks of the people. But nothing of the kind is to be seen in the United States; there society governs itself for itself. All power centers in its bosom; and scarcely an individual is to be met with who would venture to conceive, or, still less, to express, the idea of seeking it elsewhere. The nation participates in the making of its laws by the choice of its legislators, and in the execution of them by the choice of the agents of the executive government; it may almost be said to govern itself, so feeble and so restricted is the share left to the administration, so little do the authorities forget their popular origin and the power from which they emanate.

— 2 —

POLITICAL PARTIES

A. CENTRALIZED V. DECENTRALIZED PARTIES

THE CASE FOR CENTRALIZED PARTIES *

Report of the Committee on Political Parties American Political Science Association

Few questions have so agitated the minds of American political scientists as the issue of political party reform. Often with one eye cast covetously at the British system, they have frequently proposed that American parties be transformed into more disciplined and, hence, more "responsible" instruments of the public will.

In 1946 the American Political Science Association created a Committee on Political Parties to study the question. Professor E. E. Schattschneider, now emeritus of Wesleyan University, was chairman and Professor Fritz Morstein Marx, now dean of Hunter College, was chairman of the sub-committee to draft a report.

The report of the committee, excerpts from which are

* From *Toward a More Responsible Two-Party System: A Report of the Committee on Political Parties, American Political Science Association* (supplement to *American Political Science Review,* vol. XLIV, no. 3, September 1950), pp. v-vi, 5-11, and 15-25. Reprinted by permission. Members of the committee were Thomas S. Barclay, Clarence A. Berdahl, Hugh A. Bone, Franklin L. Burdette, Paul T. David, Merle Fainsod, Bertram M. Gross, E. Allen Helms, E. M. Kirkpatrick, John W. Lederle, Fritz Morstein Marx, Louise Overacker, Howard Penniman, Kirk H. Porter, E. E. Schattschneider, and J. B. Shannon.

reprinted below, has been generally recognized as a classic statement of the view of the advocates of party reform.

Historical and other factors have caused the American two-party system to operate as two loose associations of state and local organizations, with very little national machinery and very little national cohesion. As a result, either major party, when in power, is ill-equipped to organize its members in the legislative and the executive branches into a government held together and guided by the party program. Party responsibility at the polls thus tends to vanish. This is a very serious matter, for it affects the very heartbeat of American democracy. It also poses grave problems of domestic and foreign policy in an era when it is no longer safe for the nation to deal piecemeal with issues that can be disposed of only on the basis of coherent programs.

Can anything be done about it? Yes, a good many things can be done about it. In presenting suggestions, however, this publication confines itself to showing concrete lines of approach. Its authors do not believe in panaceas. Nor do they believe that organizational and procedural rearrangements by themselves work lasting changes. Real change comes from an appreciation of its need, by ordinary citizens as well as by political leaders. Such proposals for readjustment of the party machinery as are offered here are meant to meet the perfectly sensible complaint that purely negative criticism is of little use.

THE NEED FOR GREATER PARTY RESPONSIBILITY

THE ROLE OF THE POLITICAL PARTIES

1. *The Parties and Public Policy.* Throughout this report political parties are treated as indispensable instruments of government. That is to say, we proceed on the proposition that *popular government in a nation of more than 150 million people requires political parties which provide the electorate with a proper range of choice between alternatives of action.* The party system thus

serves as the main device for bringing into continuing relationship those ideas about liberty, majority rule and leadership which Americans are largely taking for granted.

For the great majority of Americans, the most valuable opportunity to influence the course of public affairs is the choice they are able to make between the parties in the principal elections. While in an election the party alternative necessarily takes the form of a choice between candidates, putting a particular candidate into office is not an end in itself. The concern of the parties with candidates, elections and appointments is misunderstood if it is assumed that parties can afford to bring forth aspirants for office without regard to the views of those so selected. Actually, the party struggle is concerned with the direction of public affairs. Party nominations are no more than a means to this end. In short, party politics inevitably involves public policy in one way or another. *In order to keep the parties apart, one must consider the relations between each and public policy.*

This is not to ignore that in the past the American two-party system has shown little propensity for evolving original or creative ideas about public policy; that it has even been rather sluggish in responding to such ideas in the public interest; that it reflects in an enlarged way those differences throughout the country which are expressed in the operation of the federal structure of government; and that in all political organizations a considerable measure of irrationality manifests itself.

Giving due weight to each of these factors, we are nevertheless led to conclude that the choices provided by the two-party system are valuable to the American people in proportion to their definition in terms of public policy. *The reasons for the growing emphasis on public policy in party politics are to be found, above all, in the very operations of modern government.* With the extraordinary growth of the responsibilities of government, the discussion of public affairs for the most part makes sense only in terms of public policy.

2. *The New Importance of Program.* One of the most pressing requirements of contemporary politics is for the party in power to furnish a general kind of direction

over the government as a whole. *The crux of public affairs lies in the necessity for more effective formulation of general policies and programs and for better integration of all of the far-flung activities of modern government.*

Only large-scale and representative political organizations possess the qualifications needed for these tasks. The ascendancy of national issues in an industrial society, the impact of the widening concern of government with problems of the general welfare, the entrance into the realm of politics of millions of new voters—all of these factors have tended to broaden the base of the parties as the largest political organizations in the country. *It is in terms of party programs that political leaders can attempt to consolidate public attitudes toward the work plans of government.*

Modern public policy, therefore, accentuates the importance of the parties, not as mere brokers between different groups and interests, but as agencies of the electorate. Because it affects unprecedented numbers of people and because it depends for its execution on extensive and widespread public support, modern public policy requires a broad political base. That base can be provided only by the parties, which reach people touched by no other political organization.

3. *The Potentialities of the Party System. The potentialities of the two-party system are suggested, on the one hand, by the fact that for all practical purposes the major parties monopolize elections; and, on the other, by the fact that both parties have in the past managed to adapt themselves to the demands made upon them by external necessities.*

Moreover, in contrast with any other political organization today in existence, the major parties even now are forced to consider public policy at least broadly enough to make it likely for them to win elections. If public esteem of the parties is much less high than it might be, the depressed state of their reputation has resulted in the main from their past indifference to broadly conceived public policy. This indifference has fixed in the popular mind the idea of spoils, patronage and plunder. It is hence not astonishing when one hears a chosen representative assert for the public ear that in his state "people put principles above party." Much of the agitation for nonpartisanship—despite the impossibility of nonpartisan organization on a national level—is rooted in the same attitudes.

Bad reputations die hard, but things are no longer what they used to be. Certainly success in presidential campaigns today is based on broad national appeals to the widest possible constituencies. To a much greater extent than in the past, elections are won by influences and trends that are felt throughout the country. *It is therefore good practical politics to reconsider party organization in the light of the changing conditions of politics.*

It appeared desirable in this report to relate the potentialities of the party system to both the conditions that confront the nation and the expected role of the parties. *Happily such an effort entails an application of ideas about the party system that are no longer unfamiliar.*

Consideration of ways and means of producing a more responsible party system leads into the hazards of political invention. This is a challenge that has usually been accepted with misgivings by political scientists, who are trained to describe what is and feel less well qualified to fashion innovations. We hope that our own effort will stimulate both other political scientists and participants in practical politics to attempt similar undertakings on their own account. Only by a continuous process of invention and adjustment can the party system be adapted to meet the needs of our day.

WHAT KIND OF PARTY SYSTEM IS NEEDED?

There is little point to talking about the American party system in terms of its deficiencies and potentialities except against a picture of what the parties ought to be. Our report would be lacking in exactness without an indication of the sort of model we have in mind.

Americans are reasonably well agreed about the purposes served by the two major parties as long as the matter is discussed in generalities. When specific questions are raised, however, agreement is much more limited. We cannot assume, therefore, a commonly shared view about the essential characteristics of the party system. But we can and must state our own view.

In brief, our view is this: *The party system that is needed must be democratic, responsible and effective* —a system that is accountable to the public, respects and expresses differences of opinion, and is able to cope with the great problems of modern government. Some of the implications warrant special statement, which is the purpose of this section.

I. A Stronger Two-party System

1. *The Need for an Effective Party System.* In an era beset with problems of unprecedented magnitude at home and abroad, it is dangerous to drift without a party system that helps the nation to set a general course of policy for the government as a whole. In a two-party system, when both parties are weakened or confused by internal divisions or ineffective organization it is the nation that suffers. When the parties are unable to reach and pursue responsible decisions, difficulties accumulate and cynicism about all democratic institutions grows.

An effective party system requires first, that the parties are able to bring forth programs to which they commit themselves and, second, that the parties possess sufficient internal cohesion to carry out these programs. In such a system, the party program becomes the work program of the party, so recognized by the party leaders in and out of the government, by the party body as a whole, and by the public. This condition is unattainable unless party institutions have been created through which agreement can be reached about the general position of the party.

Clearly such a degree of unity within the parties cannot be brought about without party procedures that give a large body of people an opportunity to share in the development of the party program. One great function of the party system is to bring about the widest possible consent in relation to defined political goals, which provides the majority party with the essential means of building public support for the policies of the government. Democratic procedures in the internal affairs of the parties are best suited to the development of agreement within each party.

2. *The Need for an Effective Opposition Party.* The argument for a stronger party system cannot be divorced from measures designed to make the parties more fully accountable to the public. *The fundamental requirement of such accountability is a two-party system in which the opposition party acts as the critic of the party in power, developing, defining and presenting the policy alternatives which are necessary for a true choice in reaching public decisions.*

Beyond that, the case for the American two-party system need not be restated here. The two-party system is so strongly rooted in the political traditions of this country and public preference for it is so well established that consideration of other possibilities seems entirely academic. When we speak of the parties without further qualification, we mean throughout our report the two major parties. The inference is not that we consider third or minor parties undesirable or ineffectual within their limited orbit. Rather, we feel that the minor parties in the longer run have failed to leave a lasting imprint upon both the two-party system and the basic processes of American government.

In spite of the fact that the two-party system is part of the American political tradition, it cannot be said that the role of the opposition party is well understood. This is unfortunate because democratic government is greatly influenced by the character of the opposition party. The measures proposed elsewhere in our report to help the party in power to clarify its policies are equally applicable to the opposition.

The opposition most conducive to responsible government is an organized party opposition, produced by the organic operation of the two-party system. When there are two parties identifiable by the kinds of action they propose, the voters have an actual choice. On the other hand, the sort of opposition presented by a coalition that cuts across party lines, as a regular thing, tends to deprive the public of a meaningful alternative. When such coalitions are formed after the elections are over, the public usually finds it difficult to understand the new situation and to reconcile it with the purpose of the ballot. Moreover, on that basis it is next to impossible to hold either party responsible for its political record. This is a serious source of public discontent.

II. Better Integrated Parties

1. *The Need for a Party System with Greater Resistance to Pressure.* As a consciously defined and consistently followed line of action keeps individuals from losing themselves in irresponsible ventures, so a program-conscious party develops greater resistance against the inroads of pressure groups.

The value of special-interest groups in a diversified society made up of countless groupings and specializations should be obvious. But organized interest groups cannot do the job of the parties. Indeed, it is only when a working formula of the public interest in its *general* character is made manifest by the parties in terms of coherent programs that the claims of interest groups can be adjusted on the basis of political responsibility. Such adjustment, once again, calls for the party's ability to honor its word.

There is little to suggest that the phenomenal growth of interest organizations in recent decades has come to its end. Organization along such lines is a characteristic feature of our civilization. To some extent these interest groups have replaced or absorbed into themselves older local institutions in that they make it possible for the government and substantial segments of the nation to maintain contact with each other. It must be obvious, however, that *the whole development makes necessary a reinforced party system that can cope with the multiplied organized pressures.* The alternative would be a scheme perhaps best described as government by pressure groups intent upon using the parties to deflect political attention from themselves.

By themselves, the interest groups cannot attempt to define public policy democratically. Coherent public policies do not emerge as the mathematical result of the claims of all of the pressure groups. The integration of the interest groups into the political system is a function of the parties. Any tendency in the direction of a strengthened party system encourages the interest groups to align themselves with one or the other of the major parties.

Such a tendency is already at work. One of the noteworthy features of contemporary American politics is the fact that not a few interest groups have found it impossible to remain neutral toward both parties. To illustrate, the entry of organized labor upon the political scene has in turn impelled antagonistic special interests to coalesce in closer political alignments.

In one respect the growth of the modern interest groups is exerting a direct effect upon the internal distribution of power within the parties. They counteract and offset local interests; they are a nationalizing influence. Indeed, the proliferation of interest groups has been one of the factors in the rise of national issues because these groups tend to organize and define their objectives on a national scale.

Parties whose political commitments count are of particular significance to interest organizations with large membership such as exist among industrial workers and farmers, but to a lesser extent also among businessmen. Unlike the great majority of pressure groups, these organizations through their membership—and in proportion to their voting strength—are able to play a measurable role in elections. Interest groups of this kind are the equivalent of organizations of voters. For reasons of mutual interest, the relationship between them and the parties tends to become explicit and continuing.

A stronger party system is less likely to give cause for the deterioration and confusion of purposes which sometimes passes for compromise but is really an unjustifiable surrender to narrow interests. *Compromise among interests is compatible with the aims of a free society only when the terms of reference reflect an openly acknowledged concept of the public interest.* There is every reason to insist that the parties be held accountable to the public for the compromises they accept.

2. *The Need for a Party System with Sufficient Party Loyalty*. It is here not suggested, of course, that the parties should disagree about everything. Parties do not, and need not, take a position on all questions that allow for controversy. The proper function of the parties is to develop and define policy alternatives on matters likely to be of interest to the whole country, on issues related

to the responsibility of the parties for the conduct of either the government or the opposition.

Needed clarification of party policy in itself will not cause the parties to differ more fundamentally or more sharply than they have in the past. The contrary is much more likely to be the case. The clarification of party policy may be expected to produce a more reasonable discussion of public affairs, more closely related to the political performance of the parties in their actions rather than their words. *Nor is it to be assumed that increasing concern with their programs will cause the parties to erect between themselves an ideological wall.* There is no real ideological division in the American electorate, and hence programs of action presented by responsible parties for the voter's support could hardly be expected to reflect or strive toward such division.

It is true at the same time that ultimately any political party must establish some conditions for membership and place some obligations on its representatives in government. Without so defining its identity the party is in danger of ceasing to be a party. To make party policy effective the *parties have the right and the duty to announce the terms to govern participation in the common enterprise.* This basic proposition is rarely denied, nor are precedents lacking. But there are practical difficulties in the way of applying restraints upon those who disregard the stated terms.

It is obvious that an effective party cannot be based merely or primarily on the expulsion of the disloyal. To impose discipline in any voluntary association is possible only as a last resort and only when a wide consensus is present within the association. Discipline and consensus are simply the front and rear sides of the same coin. *The emphasis in all consideration of party discipline must be, therefore, on positive measures to create a strong and general agreement on policies.* Thereafter, the problem of discipline is secondary and marginal.

When the membership of the party has become well aware of party policy and stands behind it, assumptions about teamwork within the party are likely to pervade the whole organization. Ultimately it is the electorate itself which will determine how firmly it wants the lines of party allegiance to be drawn. Yet even a small shift of emphasis toward party cohesion is likely to produce changes not only in the structure of the parties but also in the degree to which members identify themselves with their party.

Party unity is always a relative matter. It may be fostered, but the whole weight of tradition in American politics is against very rigid party discipline. As a general rule, the parties have a basis for expecting adherence to the party program when their position is reasonably explicit. Thus it is evident that the disciplinary difficulties of the parties do not result primarily from a reluctance to impose restraints but from the neglect of positive measures to give meaning to party programs.

As for party cohesion in Congress, the parties have done little to build up the kind of unity within the congressional party that is now so widely desired. Traditionally congressional candidates are treated as if they were the orphans of the political system, with no truly adequate party mechanism available for the conduct of their campaigns. Enjoying remarkably little national or local party support, congressional candidates have mostly been left to cope with the political hazards of their occupation on their own account. *A basis for party cohesion in Congress will be established as soon as the parties interest themselves sufficiently in their congressional candidates to set up strong and active campaign organizations in the constituencies.* Discipline is less a matter of what the parties do to their congressional candidates than what the parties do *for* them.

III. More Responsible Parties

1. *The Need for Parties Responsible to the Public. Party responsibility means the responsibility of both parties to the general public, as enforced in elections.* Responsibility of the party in power centers on the conduct of the government, usually in terms of policies. The party in power has a responsibility, broadly defined, for the general management of the government, for its manner of getting results, for the results achieved, for the consequences of inaction as well as action, for the intended and unintended outcome of its conduct of public affairs,

for all that it plans to do, for all that it might have foreseen, for the leadership it provides, for the acts of all of its agents, and for what it says as well as for what it does.

Party responsibility includes the responsibility of the opposition party, also broadly defined, for the conduct of its opposition, for the management of public discussion, for the development of alternative policies and programs, for the bipartisan policies which it supports, for its failures and successes in developing the issues of public policy, and for its leadership of public opinion. The opposition is as responsible for its record in Congress as is the party in power. It is important that the opposition party be effective but it is equally important that it be responsible, for an irresponsible opposition is dangerous to the whole political system.

Party responsibility to the public, enforced in elections, implies that there be more than one party, for the public can hold a party responsible only if it has a choice. Again, unless the parties identify themselves with programs, the public is unable to make an intelligent choice between them. The public can understand the general management of the government only in terms of policies. When the parties lack the capacity to define their actions in terms of policies, they turn irresponsible because the electoral choice between the parties becomes devoid of meaning.

As a means of achieving responsibility, the clarification of party policy also tends to keep public debate on a more realistic level, restraining the inclination of party spokesmen to make unsubstantiated statements and charges. When party policy is made clear, the result to be expected is a more reasonable and profitable discussion, tied more closely to the record of party action. When there is no clear basis for rating party performance, when party policies cannot be defined in terms of a concrete program, party debate tears itself loose from the facts. Then wild fictions are used to excite the imagination of the public.

2. *The Need for Parties Responsible to Their Members.* Party responsibility includes also the responsibility of party leaders to the party membership, as enforced in

primaries, caucuses and conventions. To this end the internal processes of the parties must be democratic, the party members must have an opportunity to participate in intraparty business, and the leaders must be accountable to the party. Responsibility demands that the parties concern themselves with the development of good relations between the leaders and the members. Only thus can the parties act as intermediaries between the government and the people. Strengthening the parties involves, therefore, the improvement of the internal democratic processes by which the leaders of the party are kept in contact with the members.

The external and the internal kinds of party responsibility need not conflict. Responsibility of party leaders to party members promotes the clarification of party policy when it means that the leaders find it necessary to explain the policy to the membership. Certainly the lack of unity within the membership cannot be overcome by the fiat of an irresponsible party leadership. A democratic internal procedure can be used not merely to test the strength of the various factions within a party but also to resolve the conflicts. The motives for enlarging the areas of agreement within the parties are persuasive because unity is the condition of success.

Intraparty conflict will be minimized if it is generally recognized that national, state and local party leaders have a common responsibility to the party membership. Intraparty conflict is invited and exaggerated by dogmas that assign to local party leaders an exclusive right to appeal to the party membership in their area.

Occasions may arise in which the parties will find it necessary to apply sanctions against a state or local party organization, especially when that organization is in open rebellion against policies established for the whole party. There are a variety of ways in which recognition may be withdrawn. It is possible to refuse to seat delegates to the National Convention; to drop from the National Committee members representing the dissident state organization; to deny legislative committee assignments to members of Congress sponsored by the disloyal organization; and to appeal directly to the party membership in the state or locality, perhaps even promoting a rival organization. The power to take strong measures is there.

It would be unfortunate, however, if the problem of party unity were thought of as primarily a matter of punishment. Nothing prevents the parties from explaining themselves to their own members. The party members have power to insist that local and state party organizations and leaders cooperate with the party as a whole; all the members need is a better opportunity to find out what party politics is about. The need for sanctions is relatively small when state and local organizations are not treated as the restricted preserve of their immediate leaders. National party leaders ought to have access to party members everywhere as a normal and regular procedure because they share with local party leaders responsibility to the same party membership. It would always be proper for the national party leaders to discuss all party matters with the membership of any state or local party organization. Considering their great prestige, wise and able national party leaders will need very little more than this opportunity.

The political developments of our time place a heavy emphasis on national issues as the basis of party programs. As a result, the party membership is coming to look to the national party leaders for a larger role in intraparty affairs. There is some evidence of growing general agreement within the membership of each party, strong enough to form a basis of party unity, provided the parties maintain close contact with their own supporters.

In particular, *national party leaders have a legitimate interest in the nomination of congressional candidates,* though normally they try hard to avoid the appearance of any intervention. Depending on the circumstances, this interest can be expressed quite sufficiently by seeking a chance to discuss the nomination with the party membership in the congressional district. On the other hand, it should not be assumed that state and local party leaders usually have an interest in congressional nominations antagonistic to the interest of the national leaders in maintaining the general party policy. As a matter of fact, congressional nominations are not considered great prizes by the local party organization as generally as one might think. It is neglect of congressional nominations and elections more than any other factor that weakens party unity in Congress. It should be added, however, that what is said here about intraparty relations with respect to congressional nominations applies also to other party nominations.

3. *The Inadequacy of the Existing Party System.* The existing party system is inadequately prepared to meet the demands now being made upon it chiefly because its central institutions are not well organized to deal with national questions. The sort of party organization needed today is indirectly suggested by the origin of the traditional party structure. This structure developed in a period in which local interests were dominant and positive governmental action at the national level did not play the role it assumed later.

PROPOSALS FOR PARTY RESPONSIBILITY

NATIONAL PARTY ORGANIZATION

I. Principal Party Bodies

1. *The National Convention.* We assume its continuation as the principal representative and deliberative organ of the party. The convention should meet at least biennially, with easy provision for special meetings. It should also cease to be a delegate convention of unwieldy size.

2. *The National Committee.* It is highly desirable for the National Convention to reassert its authority over the National Committee through a more active participation in the final selection of the committee membership. It is also desirable that the members of the National Committee reflect the actual strength of the party within the areas they represent.

3. *The Party Council.* We propose a Party Council of 50 members. Such a Party Council should consider and settle the larger problems of party management, within limits prescribed by the National Convention; propose a preliminary draft of the party platform to the National Convention; interpret the platform in relation to current problems; choose for the National Convention the group of party leaders outside the party organizations;

consider and make recommendations to appropriate party organs in respect to congressional candidates; and make recommendations to the National Convention, the National Committee or other appropriate party organs with respect to conspicuous departures from general party decisions by state or local party organizations. In presidential years, the council would naturally become a place for the discussion of presidential candidacies, and might well perform the useful function of screening these candidacies in a preliminary way. Within this Party Council there might well be a smaller group of party advisers to serve as a party cabinet.

II. Intraparty Relationships

1. *State and Local Party Organizations.* Organizational patterns of the parties are predicated on the assumption that a party committee is necessary for each electoral area. There is a growing dissatisfaction with the results of this system on the local level, especially the multiplicity of organizations. An increasing number of state legislators are noting the breakdown or lack of party responsibility and discipline and the growth of internal separatism in state government. It is necessary for both parties to reexamine their purposes and functions in the light of the present-day environment, state and local, in which they operate.

2. *Relations between National, State and Local Organizations.* Establishment of a Party Council would do much to coordinate the different party organizations, and should be pressed with that objective in mind. Regional conferences held by both parties have clearly been fruitful. Regional party organizations should be encouraged. Local party organizations should be imbued with a stronger sense of loyalty to the entire party organization and feel their responsibility for promoting the broader policies of the party. This can be done by fostering local party meetings, regularly and frequently held, perhaps monthly. The national organization may deal with conspicuous or continued disloyalty on the part of any state organization. Consideration should be given to the development of additional means of dealing with rebellious and disloyal state organizations.

3. *Headquarters and Staff.* Both parties are now aware of the need to maintain permanent headquarters, with staff equipped for research and publicity. A beginning has been made, but much still remains to be done. Staff development at party headquarters provides the essential mechanism to enable each party to concern itself appropriately with its continuing responsibilities.

PARTY PLATFORMS

I. Nature of the Platform

1. *Alternative Purposes.* Should the party platform be a statement of general principles representing the permanent or long-range philosophy of the party? Or should it state the party's position on immediate issues? Actually, the platform is usually made up of both the more permanent and the more fleeting elements.

2. *Interpretation of the Platform.* As a body representing the various parts of the party structure, the Party Council should be able to give authoritative and reasonably acceptable interpretations of the platform.

3. *National-State Platform Conflicts.* What is needed is better coordination in the declaration of party principles. The Party Council would be the appropriate party agency to interpret the respective platforms and determine the right position in case of conflict. There is very little likelihood indeed for the Party Council to be inconsiderate of arguable claims of state autonomy.

4. *Binding Character.* In spite of clear implications and express pledges, there has been much difference of opinion as to the exact binding quality of a platform. All of this suggests the need for appropriate machinery, such as a Party Council, to interpret and apply the national program in respect to doubts or details. When that is done by way of authoritative and continuing statement, the party program should be considered generally binding.

II. Problems of Platform-making

1. *Method of Formulating Party Platforms.* Occasionally the state platforms are deliberately delayed until

after the national platform has been adopted, in order to have a basis for conformity. Such practice is to be encouraged, and state legislation that prevents it ought to be changed. A method of platform-making that is closely related to the congressional as well as to the presidential campaign must be developed, and with more direct participation by the party members of Congress.

2. *Improvement of Platforms and Platform-making.* In both parties, the Platform Committee or a working part of it is now appointed some weeks in advance of the National Convention. The practice of holding public hearings on the policies to be incorporated into the platform has been fairly well established. This consultation is of importance, for it makes the parties aware of the interest in particular policies.

3. *Proposals.* Party platforms should be formulated at least every two years. National platforms should emphasize general party principles and national issues. State and local platforms should be expected to conform to the national platform on matters of general party principle or on national policies. To achieve better machinery for platform-making, the Party Council, when set up, should prepare a tentative draft well in advance of the National Convention for the consideration of the appropriate convention committee and the convention itself. Local party meetings should be held for the discussion and consideration of platform proposals.

PARTY ORGANIZATION IN CONGRESS

I. Introduction

1. *External Factors.* A higher degree of party responsibility in Congress cannot be provided merely by actions taken within Congress. Nevertheless, action within Congress can be of decisive significance.

2. *Continuous Evolution.* The materials for responsible party operations in Congress are already on hand. The key to progress lies in making a full-scale effort to use them.

II. Tightening Up the Congressional Party Organization

1. *The Leaders.* For more than ten years now the press has carried news about regular meetings between the President and the Big Four of Congress—the Speaker of the House, the Majority Leader of the House, the Vice President and the Majority Leader of the Senate, when the four are of the President's party. It would be an error to attempt to supplant the relationship between the Big Four and the President by some new body. Whenever it becomes necessary for the President to meet with the leaders of both parties in Congress, it is a simple matter for the Big Four to be expanded to six or eight. In the public eye a party leader like these is a spokesman for his party as a whole. It is necessary that there be broad consultation throughout the national leadership of a party before a party leader is elected in either house.

2. *The Leadership Committees.* We submit these proposals: In both the Senate and the House, the various leadership groups should be consolidated into one truly effective and responsible leadership committee for each party. Each of these four committees should be responsible not only for submitting policy proposals to the party membership, but also for discharging certain functions with respect to the committee structure and the legislative schedule. Each of the four committees should be selected or come up for a vote of confidence no less often than every two years. Occasion must be found reasonably often for the leadership committees of each party in the two houses to meet together. Furthermore, the rival leadership committees in each house should meet together on a more regular basis. A case can also be made for the four leadership groups to meet on specific occasions.

3. *Caucuses or Conferences.* More frequent meetings of the party membership in each house should be held. A binding caucus decision on legislative policy should be used primarily to carry out the party's principles and program. When members of Congress disregard a caucus decision taken in furtherance of national party policy, they should expect disapproval. The party leadership committees should be responsible for calling more fre-

quent caucuses or conferences and developing the agenda of points for discussion.

III. Party Responsibility for Committee Structure

1. *Selection of Committee Chairmen.* It is not playing the game fairly for party members who oppose the commitments in their party's platform to rely on seniority to carry them into committee chairmanships. Party leaders have compelling reason to prevent such a member from becoming chairman—and they are entirely free so to exert their influence. The task of party leaders, when confronted with revolt on the part of committee chairmen, is not easy. Obviously problems of this sort must be handled in the electoral process itself as well as in the congressional arena.

2. *Assignment of Members to Committees.* The slates of committee assignments should be drawn up by the party leadership committees and presented to the appropriate party caucuses for approval or modification. There is nothing sound in having the party ratio on the committees always correspond closely to the party ratio in the House itself. Committee assignments should be subjected to regular reexamination by the party caucus or conference with reasonable frequency.

3. *Committee Staff.* Staff assistance should be available to minority as well as majority members of a committee whenever they want it. Where all committee staff is controlled by the majority, a change in power threatens continuity of service.

IV. Party Responsibility for the Legislative Schedule

1. *The Need for Scheduling.* Schedules should be openly explained on the floor in advance. No committee should be in charge of legislative scheduling except the party leadership committee.

2. *House Guidance of Legislative Traffic.* A democratic approach would be to substitute open party control for control by the Rules Committee or individual chairmen.

3. *The Right to Vote in the Senate.* The present cloture rule should be amended. The best rule is one that provides for majority cloture on all matters before the Senate.

POLITICAL PARTICIPATION

Widespread political participation fosters responsibility as well as democratic control in the conduct of party affairs and the pursuit of party policies. A more responsible party system is intimately linked with the general level as well as the forms of political participation.

I. Intraparty Democracy

1. *Party Membership.* As stress is placed by the parties upon policy and the interrelationship of problems at various levels of government, association with a party should become more interesting and attractive to many who hold aloof today.

2. *Machinery of Intraparty Democracy.* If the National Convention is to serve as the grand assembly of the party, in which diverse viewpoints are compounded into a course of action, it must be nourished from below. To this end local party groups are needed that meet frequently to discuss and initiate policy.

3. *Toward a New Concept of Party Membership.* The existence of a national program, drafted at frequent intervals by a party convention both broadly representative and enjoying prestige, should make a great difference. It would prompt those who identify themselves as Republicans or Democrats to think in terms of support of that program, rather than in terms of personalities, patronage and local matters. Once machinery is established which gives the party member and his representative a share in framing the party's objectives, once there are safeguards against internal dictation by a few in positions of influence, members and representatives will feel readier to assume an obligation to support the program. Membership defined in these terms does not ask for mindless discipline enforced from above. It generates self-discipline which stems from free identification with aims one helps to define.

II. Nominating Procedures

1. *United States Senator and Representative.* Nominations for United States Senator and Representative are governed largely by state laws that vary radically in their

provisions. National regulation would overcome the disadvantages of so much variety. But one must face the practical objections to national regulation. The direct primary probably can be adapted to the needs of parties unified in terms of national policy. The closed primary deserves preference because it is more readily compatible with the development of a responsible party system. The open primary tends to destroy the concept of membership as the basis of party organization. Cross filing is bound to obscure program differences between the parties, and to eliminate any sense of real membership on the part of the rank and file. The Washington blanket primary corrupts the meaning of party even further by permitting voters at the same primary to roam at will among the parties. The formal or informal proposal of candidates by preprimary meetings of responsible party committees or party councils is a healthy development. Quite appropriately the Party Council might become a testing ground for candidates for United States Senator or Representative.

2. *Presidential Nomination.* In the National Convention, delegates representative of the party membership should be chosen by direct vote of the rank and file. The Party Council naturally would concern itself with platform plans and the relative claims of those who might be considered for presidential and vice presidential nominations. In time it may be feasible and desirable to substitute a direct, national presidential primary for the indirect procedure of the convention.

III. Elections

1. *Election of the President.* The present method of electing the President and Vice President fosters the blight of one-party monopoly and results in concentration of campaign artillery in pivotal industrial states where minority groups hold the balance of power. In the persistent agitation for change in the Electoral College system, stress should be placed both upon giving all sections of the country a real voice in electing the President and the Vice President and upon developing a two-party system in present one-party areas.

2. *Term of Representative.* It appears desirable to lengthen the term of Representative to four years.

3. *Campaign Funds.* Existing statutory limitations work toward a scattering of responsibility for the collecting of funds among a large number of independent party and nonparty committees. Repeal of these restrictions would make it possible for a national body to assume more responsibility in the field of party finance. The situation might be improved in still another way by giving a specified measure of government assistance to the parties. Everything that makes the party system more meaningful to all voters leads incidentally to a broadening of the base of financial support of the parties.

4. *Apportionment and Redistricting.* It is time to insist upon congressional districts approximately equal in population.

THE CASE AGAINST CENTRALIZED PARTIES *

By Austin Ranney

Not all political scientists concurred in the findings and recommendations of the report by the Committee on Political Parties of the American Political Science Association. One of the best-known of the replies to the report is the article by Professor Austin Ranney of the University of Illinois, which is reprinted below.

The page citations to the Committee report made in Ranney's article refer to the American Political Science Review *edition, which is abridged above.*

Every American concerned with the future of democratic government in the United States owes a considerable debt to Professor Schattschneider and the American Political Science Association's Committee on Political Parties. Their *Report,* ostensibly concerned with bringing about "fuller public appreciation of a basic weakness in the American two-party system," [1] in fact addresses itself to two of the most pressing questions confronting us: How can we in America establish a governmental system capable of performing effectively the Herculean tasks thrust upon it by the demanding times in which we live?

* From *American Political Science Review,* vol. XLV, no. 2, June 1951, pp. 488-499. Reprinted by permission.

[1] Above pp. 52-74.

And how can we make sure that such a government will at the same time be thoroughly responsible to the people? The members of the Committee appear to consider both questions to be of equal importance. The goal, they feel, must be a government which is both effective *and* democratic. And if their *Report* does nothing more than precipitate a general and serious discussion of these urgent questions, the Committee will have more than justified its existence.

The *Report* deserves the serious attention of a far wider audience than one exclusively of specialists in political parties for it takes the position that a responsible party system is the only possible institutional mechanism for providing us with effective and democratic government. Its explication of that position, its analysis of why and in what respects American parties are at present incapable of doing the job, and its prescription of remedies for their deficiencies—all these merit the most careful consideration of the political theorist and the general student of American government, as well as of the specialist in parties.

It is precisely because of agreement with the members of the Committee upon the importance of the questions raised, and because of gratitude to them for their attempt to answer these questions, that the writer feels it necessary to point out why their analysis of the problem is inadequate in certain respects. For purposes of brevity, this commentary will be confined to the two sections of the *Report* which most seriously weaken its total argument: (1) its explication of the notion of "intraparty democracy"; and (2) its analysis of why American parties are as they are and what must therefore be done in order to improve them.

I. THE IDEA OF "INTRAPARTY DEMOCRACY"

One of the ideas stressed most diligently in the *Report* is that there must be, along with the "external responsibility" of the parties to the electorate at large, also "internal responsibility," or "the responsibility of party leaders to the party membership, as enforced in primaries, caucuses and conventions." [2] "Intraparty democracy," it

[2] *Ibid.*, p. 23.

is further explained, means three things: (1) "the internal processes of the parties must be democratic," (2) "the party members must have an opportunity to participate in intraparty business," and (3) "the leaders must be accountable to the party." And not only is this "internal responsibility" as important a goal as the "external responsibility" of the parties themselves to the voters, but, the *Report* adds, the former will, by promoting closer relations between the leaders and the rank and file and by enlarging the areas of agreement within the parties, also tend to *promote* the latter.[3]

Two questions about such a conception of "intraparty democracy" immediately suggest themselves: (1) What persons should be considered "party members" whose right to participate in intraparty business should be guaranteed and to whom party leaders should be accountable? And (2) how may this "accountability" be institutionalized and made effective? The *Report* has a great deal to say about the first question, but, so far as the writer can tell, no clear and unequivocal answer emerges. The Committee comments initially:

> The vagueness of formal leadership that prevails at the top has its counterpart in the vagueness of formal membership at the bottom. *No understandings or rules or criteria exist with respect to membership in a party. . . .* It is obviously difficult, if not impossible, to secure anything like harmony of policy and action within political parties so loosely organized as this.[4]

Under our present direct primary laws, the only "rule" or "criterion" of party membership is the voter's assertion that he is a "member" of the party in which he desires to register, and, in a few states, also his promise to vote for the party's candidàtes. Many observers believe the introduction into these laws of more precise and demanding qualifications to be indispensable to the achievement of a more useful and meaningful standard of party membership. The Committee apparently does not agree, for the only reforms in the primary laws it recommends are the general adoption of the closed primary and the pro-

[3] *Idem.*

[4] *Ibid.*, p. 27 (emphasis in the original).

hibition of such practices as cross-filing in California and the blanket primary in Washington.[5]

The *Report,* in fact, does not expressly deal with the question of what would (if we could achieve it) constitute a more useful conception of party membership, except to suggest that such a conception would include a more general agreement (though by no means complete unanimity) on matters of public policy.[6] The Committee proposes to solve the problem by a series of measures designed to encourage increased "grass-roots" discussion of party policies and candidates by the rank and file; for, we are told, more discussion will produce greater party unity, and "with increased unity within the party it is likely that party membership will be given a more explicit basis." [7] The Committee apparently hopes that the party "members" will talk themselves into such a degree of agreement that it will be unnecessary to face the difficult and unpleasant problem of whether a "member," who after full discussion with his fellow "members" is still not willing to go along with the policies and candidates the party majority has settled on, continues to have the "right" to participate in its deliberations.

The original question thus remains unanswered. We have not been told *who* has a right to be considered a party member. Yet this consideration is fundamental to the committee's notion of "intraparty democracy"; for, if the members are to have the "right" of holding party leaders to account "in primaries, caucuses and conventions," we must first know just who will be permitted to exercise this "right." Will the party leaders, for example, be "responsible" to all those persons who register as

[5] *Ibid.,* pp. 70-72. It is difficult to see the relevance of these proposed reforms to either "internal" or "external" responsibility. Is there any evidence to suggest, for example, that Senator Knowland (from a cross-filing State) and Senator Magnuson (from a blanket-primary State disagree with and stray from the programs and positions of their respective parties more than, say, Senator Morse, Senator Tobey, or ex-Senator Elmer Thomas (all from closed-primary States)?

[6] *Ibid.,* p. 69.

[7] *Ibid.,* pp. 65-70.

party members and vote in the closed primaries? Or will they be "responsible" to all those persons who vote for the party ticket?

The Committee does not clearly state its adherence to either of these concepts of party membership; but its discussion, in another part of the *Report,* of the "unrepresentativeness" of the National Conventions strongly suggests an inclination toward the ticket-voter conception. As evidence of that "unrepresentativeness," the *Report* cites the fact that the "rank and file" strength of both parties is not truly represented in the National Conventions because the number of delegates each State sends to them is based, not upon the number of voters for the party in the State, but upon the number of presidential electors it has, modified only by a certain number of additional delegates at large. To clinch the argument the *Report* quotes figures showing the great variations from delegation to delegation in each party convention in the number of party voters per delegate.[8] This argument clearly rests upon the premise that party conventions *should* represent those who vote for the party's ticket. And, if this argument about the National Conventions indicates its real position on the matter, the Committee apparently believes that anyone who votes for a party's national ticket must be regarded as a "member" of that party, one who must be "represented" in its decision-making bodies if real "intraparty democracy" is to exist.

If this is indeed what the Committee means by "membership" in a party, "intraparty democracy" seems very far away, however much discussion may go on among such "members." As Professor E. E. Schattschneider has previously argued, such individuals can be called party "members" by courtesy only, for they assume no real obligation to the party, and the party in turn has no control over them. This is not true, he points out, of the relationship between any other organization and its members. In actuality, such "members" can hardly hope to exert any more effective control of the party leaders than rooters for the New York Yankees can exert over the operations of the team—and for the same reasons.[9] If

[8] *Ibid.,* pp. 28-29.
[9] *Party Government* (New York, 1942), pp. 53-57.

we operate in terms of such a conception of party membership, in other words, it seems very likely that Michels' familiar "iron law of oligarchy" will obtain: the control of the parties will remain in the hands of those who assume some real obligation to them, and "intraparty democracy"—so far as the ticket-voting "members" are concerned—will remain only a slogan.[10]

The reader cannot be certain, however, just what the Committee regards as the requirements and obligations (if any) of party membership and how those requirements and obligations should be enforced. The *Report's* lack of clarity on this point notably affects its answer to the question of how the accountability of the leaders to the "members" is to be made effective. The "machinery of intraparty democracy" which it proposes consists of a biennial National Convention "broadly and directly representative of the rank and file of the party," and the encouragement of the discussion of issues and the suggestion of policies to the proposed Party Council by local party groups that meet frequently.[11]

But the only specific item of machinery suggested whereby the rank and file can hold the leaders *responsible* is the closed primary; and there is little evidence to suggest that, where it is employed, this institution has greatly increased "intraparty democracy" as the Committee seems to visualize it.[12]

Perhaps the primary cause of the obscurity of the Committee's argument on this whole point is its failure to make clear just what it means by "democracy" in this context. In its preliminary argument for the desirability of more responsible parties as a way of achieving a greater degree of democracy in the United States, the Committee (although the point is not made explicit) seems to regard "democracy" in the community at large as necessarily consisting in the popular choice between alternate ruling-groups, not as popular *participation* in its day-to-day

[10] Cf. Robert Michels, *Political Parties: A Sociological Study of the Oligarchical Tendencies of Modern Democracy* (Eden and Cedar Paul trans.; London, 1915) *passim.*

[11] *Report,* pp. 67-68.

[12] Cf. Schattschneider, *op. cit.,* pp. 56-58.

processes.[13] Yet its idea of "democracy" inside the parties seems to include participation as well as control. Whatever it means, one may ask, with Professor Schattschneider, if it is possible for twenty-seven million Democrats to "participate" in the close supervision of the affairs of the Democratic party any more effectively than 150 million Americans can "participate" in the close supervision of their government. "Will it be necessary," he further asks, "to develop parties within the parties in order to simplify and define the alternatives for the members?" [14]

Finally, it is difficult to see how the Committee's notion of "intraparty democracy" is calculated to promote the achievement of its other goal, the "external" responsibility of the parties to the whole community. The *Report* argues that "intraparty democracy" will promote party responsibility by increasing the unity of the members of each party behind their respective programs, but the Committee does not seem to recognize the possibilities for promoting factionalism in the parties by trying to make them into something other than purely private associations. Professor Schattschneider, for one, has argued that we can hope for more genuinely responsible parties in the United States only when their essentially *private* nature is recognized:

> Will the parties be less responsive to the needs of the voters if their private character is generally recognized? Probably not. The parties do not need laws to make them sensitive to the wishes of the voters any more than we need laws compelling merchants to please their customers. The sovereignty of the voter consists in his freedom of choice just as the sovereignty of the consumer in the economic system consists in his freedom to trade in a competitive market. That is enough; little can be added to it by inventing an imaginary membership in a fictitious party association. Democracy is not to be found *in* the parties but *between* the parties.[15]

Perhaps the Committee has a reply to this argument; but the *Report* does not provide it. Until we know what that

[13] Cf. *Report,* p. 15.
[14] *Op. cit.,* p. 58.
[15] *Ibid.,* p. 60 (emphasis in the original).

reply is, we must receive the assertion that "internal responsibility" will promote "external responsibility" with considerable reservation.

II. WHY ARE AMERICAN PARTIES AS THEY ARE?

A considerable portion of the *Report* is devoted to the suggestion of a number of reforms for American parties, all intended to make them more responsible. The Committee apparently regards the primary function of its *Report* to be that of showing the politicians and the people some practical ways and means of obtaining these goals. The validity of its program of reform however, depends upon its answer to the logically prior question of *why* American parties at present display what the Committee regards as their unsatisfactory characteristics —for does not the soundness of any therapeutic regimen depend upon the accuracy of the diagnosis upon which it is based?

Most present-day students of the American party system believe that the primary determinant of its nature is the fact that it must operate within a constitutional system that sets up too many and too effective barriers to the development of unified and responsible parties.[16] The *Report* begins its explanation as though it too were going to follow the orthodox course. "Party institutions and their operations," we are told, "cannot be divorced from the general conditions that govern the nature of the party system."[17] The paragraphs that follow, however, do not suggest what general *conditions* "govern" the nature of American parties; instead the Committee lists certain *characteristics* of the parties which it considers undesirable: generally, localism, the absence of any effective central leadership, and the ambiguity of membership; more specifically, the inadequacy of the national party

[16] Cf. *ibid.*, pp. 7-10, 123-128; V. O. Key, *Politics, Parties and Pressure Groups* (2nd ed.; New York, 1947), pp. 664-667; P. H. Odegard and E. A. Helms, *American Politics* (2nd ed.; New York, 1947), pp. 124-131; and D. D. McKean, *Party and Pressure Politics* (Boston, 1949), pp. 29-49.

[17] *Report*, p. 26.

organs and platforms, the absence of "intraparty democracy," and the failure of the parties to carry on party research.[18] Thus we are told a great deal, here and elsewhere, about the respects in which American parties are unsatisfactory, but nowhere in the *Report* is there an explicit statement of the reasons for their deficiencies.

An explanation of the unsatisfactory nature of American parties, however, is strongly implied in the Committee's position upon the *kind* of reforms needed to achieve responsible parties. They begin by rejecting any wholesale constitutional change, such as, for example, the adoption of a cabinet system. Such a system, they argue, presupposes the existence of strong parties but does not always produce them; and if we should achieve strong parties in the United States, cabinet government would be unnecessary. So the indicated program of reform is one that concentrates solely on changing the parties; when they are made more responsible, the Committee feels, the constitutional system will not seriously retard the achievement of truly effective and democratic government—

> it is easy to overestimate . . . the rigidity of the existing constitutional arrangements in the United States. Certainly the roles of the President and Congress are defined by the Constitution in terms that leave both free to cooperate and to rely on the concept of party responsibility . . . It is logical first to find out what can be done under present conditions to invigorate the parties before accepting the conclusion that *action has to begin with changing a constitutional system that did not contemplate the growing need for party responsibility when it was set up.*[19]

The *Report,* then, clearly rejects the notion that the nature of American parties is basically determined by our constitutional system. It agrees with Professor Schattschneider that

> The greatest difficulties in the way of the development of party government in the United States have been intellectual, not legal . . . (and that) . . . once a respect-

[18] *Ibid.*, pp. 26-31.
[19] *Ibid.*, pp. 35-36 (emphasis added).

> able section of the public understands the issue (sic), ways of promoting party government through the Constitution can be found.[20]

As the Committee puts it, "The character of this publication is explained by the conviction of its authors that the weakness of the American two-party system can be overcome as soon as a substantial part of the electorate wants it overcome." [21] And the electorate, they feel, *will* want the party system made stronger as soon as they fully *understand* that more responsible parties, as the Committee defines them, will produce the more effective and more democratic government which they so strongly desire.

The Committee's position on the fundamental questions of what barriers now exist against the achievement of responsible party government in the United States and how the Committee may contribute to their removal may therefore be reduced to these propositions: (1) Americans want effective and democratic government; (2) a responsible two-party system will, despite the Constitution, produce such a government; (3) the present weakness of our parties is basically a result of the fact that the people do not understand that a more responsible party system will produce the kind of government they want; (4) therefore, the way to remedy the present unsatisfactory situation is to educate the people to the possibilities of a responsible two-party system, and to start reforming the parties themselves without attempting the difficult and probably unnecessary task of formally amending the Constitution. Of the many specific reforms the *Report* proceeds to suggest, all but three are concerned solely with party matters and would require no change in the formal constitutional system.[22]

[20] *Op. cit.*, pp. 209-210.

[21] *Report*, p. v.

[22] The three exceptions are: revising the operation of the Electoral College so that the percentage of electoral votes a candidate receives will reflect his share of the popular vote (p. 74); lengthening the term of members of the House of Representatives to four years (p. 75); and introducing the short ballot principle into state elections (p. 77).

The Committee's whole position upon the question of why American parties are as they are—and consequently its whole program for reforming them—rests upon the validity of propositions (1) and (3) above. It is therefore necessary at this point to examine those propositions more critically than the Committee has done in its *Report.* Two questions that arise in this regard are: How long have American parties displayed what the Committee regards as their unsatisfactory characteristics? And does there seem to be any significant tendency for them to change in those respects? The *Report* gives somewhat ambivalent answers to both questions. There have been great changes in American society over the past fifty years, we are told, and the party system has reflected those changes—although it is not made clear in just what respects the party system has changed. "Despite these tendencies toward change, however," the *Report* continues, "*formal party organization in its main features is still substantially what it was before the Civil War* . . . The result is that the parties are now probably the most archaic institutions in the United States." [23]

But is it only *organizationally* that the parties have remained the same? Have they changed greatly with respect to what the Committee considers to be their basic deficiencies: decentralization and localism, fragmentation of leadership, ambiguity of membership, inability to hold their lines on matters of public policy, etc.? The evidence strongly suggests that in these respects they have *not* changed significantly. It is illuminating, in this connection, to examine the writings on parties produced by leading American scholars of the past seventy-five years. Such political scientists as Woodrow Wilson, Henry Jones Ford, A. Lawrence Lowell, Jesse Macy, M. I. Ostrogorski, Herbert Croly and J. Allen Smith described the American party system of 1875-1915 in almost exactly the same terms that the Committee employs to describe the parties of 1950. And the first statistical evidence of the weakness of party lines in Congress and the state legislatures was

[23] *Ibid.*, p. 25 (emphasis in the original).

provided by the famous and still relevant study of party-voting which Lowell made in 1902.[24]

If the nature of American parties has remained largely the same, it next becomes necessary to understand *why* this is so. Although the Committee does not enlighten us on this point, it might be argued that American parties have remained decentralized and irresponsible because the people have not, until very recently, been told of the desirability of a more responsible system. Yet an examination of the literature on parties produced fifty years ago soon show the inaccuracy of such an argument. Some of the most prominent writers of that time, notably Wilson, Lowell, Ford, and Frank J. Goodnow, presented a case for a more responsible American two-party system that was at least as convincing as any made today.[25] It received, moreover, a very wide hearing.[26] The inescapable fact is that the people and the politicians have been exposed to the doctrine of responsible party government (and to its criticism of American parties) for at least sixty-five years, but that the essential nature of our party system has remained the same. However one may deplore that system, he must concede that it has displayed, if nothing else, a very impressive ability to survive. The Committee's inarticulate premise that it has survived because the people have not "understood" that responsible parties will give them the kind of government they want, would be more convincing if, having made it articulate, they had adduced some evidence to support it. The as-

[24] "The Influence of Party upon Legislation in England and America," *Annual Report of the American Historical Association for the Year 1901* (Washington, D.C., 1902), Vol. 1, pp. 321-542.

[25] Cf., for example, the present writer's discussion of "Goodnow's Theory of Politics," *Southwestern Social Science Quarterly,* Vol. 30, pp. 268-276 (March, 1950).

[26] Note, in illustration of this point, the fact that Wilson's *Congressional Government,* which was first published in 1885 and was a strong defense of the doctrine of responsible party government as applied to the American party system, went through twenty-five impressions, the last of which appeared in 1925. And even as President, Wilson continued to argue for more responsible parties.

sumption that of course the people don't understand, because if they did they would demand responsible parties, is hardly borne out by the presently available evidence.

Fifty-odd years ago, A. Lawrence Lowell suggested another explanation of the resistance of American parties to change which the authors of the *Report* might well ponder.[27] His thesis was that American parties are the way they are because they are entirely appropriate to the kind of government the American people want. He developed it thus: Unified, disciplined and responsible parties are appropriate *only* to a government which seeks to locate *full* public power in the hands of popular majorities. England is the leading example of such a government, and the English people have quite properly established a cabinet system in order to enable responsible parties and majority rule to flourish; for "if the object of government is to divide the people into two political parties, and to give rapid and unlimited effect to the opinions of the majority, no better political system has ever, perhaps, been suggested. . . ." [28] A responsible party system, in short, is indispensable to a system of "unlimited" majority rule. To any other system it is quite inappropriate.

In the United States, Lowell continued, the people want majority rule only up to a point and within very definite limits:

> It is here considered of the first importance to protect the individual, to prevent the majority from oppressing the minority, and, except within certain definite limits, to give effect to the wishes of the people only after such solemn formalities have been complied with as to make it clear that popular feeling is not caused by temporary excitement, but is the result of a mature and lasting opinion.[29]

Americans, that is to say, want *both* majority rule *and* minority rights; but they feel that the former must never

[27] *Essays on Government* (Boston, 1897), particularly in the essays entitled "Cabinet Responsibility and the Constitution" and "Democracy and the Constitution."

[28] *Ibid.*, pp. 21-22.

[29] *Ibid.*, p. 22.

be allowed to abridge the latter, and that the latter should constitute a fundamental limitation upon the former. Furthermore, Americans believe that there must be far more effective restraints upon the majority than are imposed simply by trusting them to behave with self-restraint. It was to institutionalize just this set of ideas about government, Lowell explained, that the Founding Fathers wrote the kind of Constitution they did—a Constitution planned to make it as difficult as possible for any bare popular majority (or any party or "faction" representing such a majority) to command the *whole* power of the government. Thus the framers divided the power of the national government among three different agencies, no one of which has full power. They made each of these agencies independent of the others by having it derive its power from a different source and acquire its personnel by a different mode of selection. And they provided that the enormously important power of making the final decision upon the limits of the powers of various agencies and of the government as a whole be given to the body furthest removed from control by bare popular majorities—the courts of law.[30] The Founding Fathers did *not* create this elaborate and complex structure for the reason which the *Report* suggests, i.e., because they "did not contemplate the growing need for party responsibility when (the Constitution) was set up."[31] They did it because they wanted to make sure that no unified and disciplined majority "faction" would ever be able to trample upon the rights of minorities; and the only sure way to prevent such a situation seemed to be to give any substantial minority the power to protect itself by vetoing any act of any majority it sees fit to veto.

But where does the American party system fit into such a scheme of government? American parties *as they exist,* said Lowell, are not only appropriate to it, but they are of considerable help in making it work. For one thing, he pointed out, our decentralized and irresponsible parties make it difficult for strong-willed and self-conscious popular majorities even to form. The American party leader

[30] *Ibid.,* pp. 90-104.
[31] *Report,* p. 36.

thus does not seek to rally a strong popular majority around a concrete and consistent program of public policy; instead

> he usually attempts, on the contrary, to conciliate all classes and delights in such language as "a tariff for revenue only, so adjusted as to protect American industries"; an expression intended to win the votes of free-traders without offending the protectionists. He is a member of an army of office-seekers, whose warfare is not directed against private rights, or the interests of particular classes, or even against what might be considered crying abuses, but is waged chiefly with a rival army of office-seekers. . . . The result is, that party agitation in America does not in general involve any threat against the property or rights of private persons, and that those statutes which may be classed as socialistic rarely find a place in party programmes, and are not carried by party votes. *This state of things is not an accident. It is the natural consequence of the political system of the United States.*[32]

Elsewhere Lowell showed how American parties distort the expression of what majority opinions do exist, and how their irresponsibility and weak party lines keep even distorted majority opinions from being translated into governmental action.[33] They are, he argued, but one more aspect, albeit it an important one, of a *total* system of anti-majoritarian government, sustained by the conviction of the American people that "unlimited" popular majorities are a constant and dangerous threat to minority rights, the security of which is the primary desideratum of good government. To compare the American party system unfavorably with a model system based upon British party practices is therefore pointless, he added; for British parties are an integral part of a governmental system aimed at quite different goals than those the American system seeks to realize. So long as Americans continue to refuse to place minority rights at the mercy of bare popular majorities, Lowell concluded, the American

[32] Lowell, *Essays on Government,* pp. 107-108 (emphasis added).

[33] *Public Opinion and Popular Government* (New York, 1913), pp. 65-66, 96-97, 105, 139-140.

system of government, *including* its present system of irresponsible parties, is not likely to change.

It is by no means necessary to accept Lowell's analysis in its entirety to realize that he raised a number of questions which, whether the Committee recognizes it or not, lie at the heart of the problems with which it deals. What is the nature of democratic government? And do the American people really want such a government? Only *after* we have answered these questions can we decide what kind of party system is appropriate for the United States.

Perhaps the most valuable contribution of Lowell's discussion is his clear presentation of the necessity of a *choice* between majority rule and minority rights, and his reminder that the doctrine of responsible party government makes sense only in a context where the former has been chosen. His analysis serves to show us that, unless we are willing to leave it to the good will and sense of self-restraint of bare popular majorities, the protection of minority rights necessarily involves giving some agency *external to* such majorities and *not responsible to* them the power to veto any act of a majority which it disapproves. We must, if "minority rights" in that sense is our choice, enable the minorities both to determine the boundaries of their rights *and* to have the final say as to whether any given act of a majority transgresses those boundaries. We must furthermore recognize that the power to veto is the power to *rule,* however we may wish to soften that harsh fact verbally; for the power to veto is the power to select the status quo from among the many alternative policies a government might, in any given situation, pursue. We must, in short, decide whether democracy to us means majority rule *or* minority rights. We cannot have both, for the latter in essence means minority *rule.*[34]

In the writer's opinion, the issues involved in the majority rule *vs.* minority rights controversy are not, and

[34] For an able recent statement, by one of its leading American exponents, of what is involved in the majoritarian position, see Willmoore Kendall, "Prolegomena to Any Future Work on Majority Rule," *Journal of Politics,* Vol. 12, pp. 694-713 (Nov., 1950).

have not been, as clearly seen and faced by the American people as Lowell seems to have believed; and the people therefore cannot be said to have made the clear choice of minority "rights" that he attributed to them. Probably the prevailing attitude in the United States is that we want *both* majority rule *and* inviolable minority rights, and that neither deserves any priority over the other.[35]

Certainly the Committee makes no clear choice, as its reluctance to make a clear statement about the position of dissident minorities within "responsible" parties shows. In the *Report's* discussion of "intraparty democracy" and the proper nature and sources of party discipline, the whole emphasis is upon the "generally (sic) binding" nature of party platforms and caucus decisions; and for the most part their explanation of the proper nature of party discipline consists of showing how fine it would be if all party members would argue themselves into agreement on program and candidates so that there would *be* few dissidents.[36] Their proposals for creating party "unity" are thus designed to build it up, not by any system of forcing members of party minorities to choose (as they must, for example, in England) between going along with the decisions of the party majority or getting out of the party, but by a series of "positive measures" for discussion, by which the Committee apparently hopes that all factions in the party will argue themselves into agreement and that the problem of the relative rights of majorities and minorities seldom need arise.[37] The *Report*

[35] This, of course, is difficult of final proof. The writer has derived his strong impression that his statement is valid from discussions of the issues with students, his understanding of the present academic and popular literature on the nature of democracy, and his interpretation of the significance of the general American belief in the desirability of such an institution as judicial review. Whether or not this statement is accurate, however, it is at least clear that Americans are not generally committed to a belief in the desirability of "unlimited" majority rule. And that, for the purposes of the argument that follows in the text, is the important point.

[36] Cf. *Report,* pp. 52-53, 61.

[37] *Ibid.,* pp. 20-22.

never tells us, however, how a "democratically organized" party should handle a situation in which the party majority has decided to do something with which a party minority cannot "conscientiously" agree.

Whatever the Committee believes democracy requires, it seems clear that only when the American people have clearly faced the necessity of choosing between majority rule and minority veto-power will we be able to tell whether Lowell's judgment of their preference for the latter is valid. And only then will we be able to predict the popular reception likely to be accorded the doctrine of responsible party government in the United States.

The authors of the *Report,* however, apparently feel that it is both possible and necessary to "sell" the people on the desirability of a "more responsible" party system without dealing with such "theoretical" matters as majority rule and minority rights and such "impractical" questions as that of constitutional revision. They must be reminded, in this connection, that their conception of a responsible party system is a *model* (not something which actually exists in this country), and a *democratic* model. It is founded upon the conviction that only *parties,* not individuals, can effectively be held responsible by the electorate for the manner in which the government is carried on. It is therefore necessary, if genuinely responsible parties are to exist, for the party which wins a *majority* of the popular votes to secure thereby the *full* power of the government. If the majority party does not exercise full power, it can hardly be held fully responsible for whatever the government does or fails to do; for is it not an axiom of contemporary political science that responsibility depends upon the possession of power? Yet a people which is not "sold" upon the idea of majority rule can hardly be "sold" a way of making majority rule effective. And a people which believes that unrestrained popular majorities cannot be trusted to rule wisely and well, is likely to continue to consider such majority-restraining traits of its party system as "independence" desirable attributes of statesmanship. A majoritarian party system, as Lowell so ably pointed out, is not likely to flourish in an anti-majoritarian governmental system. And what is much more pertinent, a majoritarian party system is not likely to be acclaimed by a people which is not sure that majority-rule democracy is what it wants.

In short, if the Committee really wishes to see genuinely effective *and* democratic government achieved in the United States, it must, however "impractical" it may seem, work for popular acceptance of the *whole* package of majority-rule democracy; it is highly impractical to plead just for a responsible party system, which after all is just one part of the total democratic package—and one which logically comes rather late in the argument. No matter how much the President and Congress may wish to "cooperate," a responsible party system can hardly flourish in a constitutional system where it is possible for a small bloc of Senators to filibuster to death any part of the winning party's program, where it is impossible, because of the staggered calendar of elections, to replace the *entire* government at any one election, and where, most important of all, a Supreme Court selected for life and largely beyond the reach of any popular majority can, for all practical purposes, declare any of the majority party's leading measures null and void.

The problem we face is not one of deciding whether the constitutional system or the parties should be changed "first." The point is that the same popular beliefs about government which sustain our present anti-majoritarian constitutional system will continue to sustain (as they have for a very long time) our anti-majoritarian party system. Only when the American people have fully accepted the doctrine of majority-rule democracy can the doctrine of responsible party government expect to receive the popular acclaim which, whether in Lowell's time or our own, it has so far been denied.

B. PARTY PLATFORMS

In retrospect 1932 looms as a turning point in American political history. A comparison of the campaign pledges of the two major parties in that key year and a grasp of the ideological distance traveled by them since then assists in understanding the role of the party platform, the nature of the Presidential campaign, and the character of the parties.

THE REPUBLICAN PARTY PLATFORM, 1932

Introduction. We, the representatives of the Republican party, in convention assembled, renew our pledge to the principles and traditions of our party and dedicate it anew to the service of the nation.

We meet in a period of widespread distress and of an economic depression that has swept the world. The emergency is second only to that of a great war. The human suffering occasioned may well exceed that of a period of actual conflict.

The supremely important problem that challenges our citizens and governments alike is to break the back of the depression, to restore the economic life of the nation and to bring encouragement and relief to the thousands of American families that are sorely afflicted.

The people themselves, by their own courage, their own patient and resolute effort in the readjustment of their own affairs, can and will work out the cure. It is our task as a party, by leadership and a wise determination of policy, to assist that recovery.

To that task we pledge all that our party possesses in capacity, leadership, resourcefulness and ability. Republicans collectively and individually in Nation and State hereby enlist in a war which will not end until the promise of American life is once more fulfilled.

Leadership. For nearly three years the world has endured an economic depression of unparalleled extent and severity. The patience and courage of our people have been severely tested, but their faith in themselves, in their institutions, and in their future remains unshaken. When victory comes, as it will, this generation will hand on to the next a great heritage unimpaired.

This will be due in large measure to the quality of the leadership that this country has had during this crisis. We have had in the White House a leader,—wise, courageous, patient, understanding, resourceful, ever-present at his post of duty, tireless in his efforts, and unswervingly faithful to American principles and ideals.

At the outset of the depression, when no man could foresee its depth and extent, the President succeeded in averting much distress by securing agreement between industry and labor to maintain wages and by stimulating programs of private and governmental construction. Throughout the depression unemployment has been limited by the systematic use of part-time employment as a substitute for the general discharge of employees. Wage scales have not been reduced except under compelling necessity. As a result there have been fewer strikes and less social disturbance than during any similar period of hard times.

The suffering and want occasioned by the great drought of 1930 were mitigated by the prompt mobilization of the resources of the Red Cross and of the government. During the trying winters of 1930-31 and 1931-32 a nation-wide organization to relieve distress was brought into being under the leadership of the President. By the spring of 1931 the possibility of a business upturn in the United States was clearly discernible when, suddenly, a train of events was set in motion in Central Europe which moved forward with extraordinary rapidity and violence, threatening the credit structure of the world, and eventually dealing a serious blow to this country.

The President foresaw the danger. He sought to avert it by proposing a suspension of inter-governmental debt payments for one year, with the purpose of relieving the pressure at the point of greatest intensity. But the credit machinery of the nations of Central Europe could not withstand the strain, and the forces of disintegration continued to gain momentum until in September Great Britain was forced to depart from the gold standard. This momentous event, followed by a tremendous raid on the dollar, resulted in a series of bank suspensions in this country, and the hoarding of currency on a large scale.

Again the President acted. Under his leadership the National Credit Association came into being. It mobilized our banking resources, saved scores of banks from failure, helped restore confidence, and proved of inestimable value in strengthening the credit structure.

By the time the Congress met, the character of our problems was clearer than ever. In his message to Congress, the President outlined a constructive and definite program which in the main has been carried out; other portions may yet be carried out.

The Railroad Credit Corporation was created. The capital of the Federal Land Banks was increased. The Reconstruction Finance Corporation came into being, and brought protection to millions of depositors, policy holders and others. Legislation was enacted enlarging the discount facilities of the Federal Reserve System; and, without reducing the legal reserves of the Federal Reserve Banks, releasing a billion dollars of gold, a formidable protection against raids on the dollar, and a greatly enlarged basis for an expansion of credit. An earlier distribution to depositors in closed banks has been brought about through the action of the Reconstruction Finance Corporation. Above all, the national credit has been placed in an impregnable position by provision for adequate revenue and a program of drastic curtailment of expenditures. All of these measures were designed to lay a foundation for the resumption of business and increased employment. But delay and the constant introduction and consideration of new and unsound measures has kept the country in a state of uncertainty and fear, and offset much of the good otherwise accomplished.

The President has recently supplemented his original program. To provide for distress, to stimulate the revival of business and employment, and to improve the agricultural situation, he recommended extending the authority of the Reconstruction Finance Corporation to enable it:

(a) To make loans to political subdivisions of public bodies or private corporations for the purpose of starting construction of income-producing or self-liquidating projects which will at once increase employment;

(b) to make loans upon security of agricultural commodities so as to insure the carrying of normal stocks of those commodities, and thus stabilize their loan value and price levels;

(c) to make loans to the Federal Farm Board to enable extension of loans to farm cooperatives and loans for export of agricultural commodities to quarters unable otherwise to purchase them;

(d) to loan up to $300,000,000 to such states as are unable to meet the calls made on them by their citizens for distress relief.

The President's program contemplates an attack on a broad front, with far-reaching objectives, but entailing no danger to the budget. The Democratic program, on the other hand, contemplates a heavy expenditure of public funds, a budget unbalanced on a large scale, with a doubtful attainment of at best a strictly limited objective.

We strongly endorse the President's program.

Unemployment and Relief. True to American traditions and principles of government the administration has regarded the relief problem as one of State and local responsibility. The work of local agencies, public and private, has been coordinated and enlarged on a nation-wide scale under the leadership of the President. Sudden and unforeseen emergencies such as the drought have been met by the Red Cross and the government. The United States Public Health Service has been of inestimable benefit to stricken areas.

There has been magnificent response and action to relieve distress by citizens, organizations and agencies public and private throughout the country.

To provide against the possible failure of local and State agencies, the President has urged the Congress to create an emergency relief fund to be loaned temporarily to any State on a showing of actual need and temporary failure of its financial resources.

The Republican party endorses this record and policy and is opposed to the Federal government entering directly into the field of private charity and direct relief to the individual.

Public Economy. Constructive plans for financial stabilization cannot be completely organized until our National, State and Municipal governments not only balance their budgets, but curtail their current expenses as well to a level which can be steadily and economically maintained for some years to come.

We urge prompt and drastic reduction of public expenditure and resistance to every appropriation not demonstrably necessary to the performance of the essential functions of government, national or local.

The Dollar. The Republican party established and will continue to uphold the gold standard and will oppose any measure which will undermine the government's credit or impair the integrity of our national currency. Relief by currency inflation is unsound in principle and dishonest in results. The dollar is impregnable in the marts of the world to-day and must remain so. An ailing body cannot be cured by quack remedies. This is no time to experiment upon the body politic or financial.

Banks and the Banking System. The efficient functioning of our economic machinery depends in no small measure on the aid rendered to trade and industry by our banking system. There is need of revising the banking laws so as to place our banking structure on a sounder basis generally for all concerned, and for the better protection of the depositing public there should be more stringent supervision and broader powers vested in the supervising authorities. We advocate such a revision.

One of the serious problems affecting our banking system has arisen from the practice of organizing separate corporations under and controlled by the same interests as banks, but participating in operations which the banks themselves are not permitted legally to undertake. We favor requiring reports of and subjecting to thorough and periodic examination all such affiliates of member banks until adequate information has been acquired on the basis of which this problem may definitely be solved in a permanent manner.

International Conference. We favor the participation by the United States in an international conference to consider matters relating to monetary questions, including the position of silver, exchange problems, and commodity prices, and possible cooperative action concerning them.

Home Loan Discount Bank System. The present Republican administration has initiated legislation for the creation of a system of Federally supervised Home Loan Discount Banks, designed to serve the home owners of all parts of the country and to encourage home ownership by making possible long-term credits for homes on more stable and more favorable terms.

There has arisen in the last few years a disturbing trend away from home ownership. We believe that everything possible should be done by governmental agencies, national, State and local, to reverse this tendency; to aid home owners by encouraging better methods of home financing; and to relieve the present inequitable tax burden on the home. In the field of national legislation we pledge that the measures creating a home-loan discount system will be pressed in Congress until adopted.

Agriculture. Farm distress in America has its root in the enormous expansion of agricultural production during the war, the deflation of 1919, 1920, and the dislocation of markets after the war. There followed, under Republican administrations, a long record of legislation in aid of the cooperative organization of farmers and in providing farm credit. The position of agriculture was gradually improved. In 1928 the Republican party pledged further measures in aid of agriculture, principally tariff protection for agricultural products and the creation of a Federal Farm Board "clothed with the necessary power to promote the establishment of a farm marketing system of farmer-owned and controlled stabilization corporations."

Almost the first official act of President Hoover was the calling of a special session of Congress to redeem these party pledges. They have been redeemed.

The 1930 Tariff Act increased the rates on agricultural

products by thirty per cent, upon industrial products only twelve per cent. That act equalized, so far as legislation can do so, the protection afforded the farmer with the protection afforded industry and prevented a vast flood of cheap wool, grain, livestock, dairy and other products from entering the American market.

By the Agricultural Marketing Act, the Federal Farm Board was created and armed with broad powers and ample funds. The object of that act, as stated in its preamble, was—"To promote the effective merchandising of agricultural commodities in interstate and foreign commerce so that . . . agriculture will be placed on the basis of economic equality with other industries . . . By encouraging the organization of producers into effective association under their own control . . . and by promoting the establishment of a farm marketing system of producer-owned and producer-controlled cooperative associations."

The Federal Farm Board, created by the Agricultural Marketing Act, has been compelled to conduct its operations during a period in which all commodity prices, industrial as well as agricultural, have fallen to disastrous levels, a period of decreasing demand and of national calamities such as drought and flood has intensified the problem of agriculture. Nevertheless, after only a little more than two years' efforts the Federal Farm Board has many achievements of merit to its credit. It has increased the membership of cooperative farm marketing associations to coordinate efforts of the local associations. By cooperation with other Federal agencies, it has made available to farm marketing associations a large value of credit, which, in the emergency, would not have otherwise been available. Larger quantities of farm products have been handled cooperatively than ever before in the history of the cooperative movement. Grain crops have been sold by the farmer through his association directly upon the world market.

Due to the 1930 Tariff Act and the Agricultural Marketing Act, it can truthfully be stated that the prices received by the American farmer for his wheat, corn, rye, barley, oats, flaxseed, cattle, butter and many other products, cruelly low though they are, are higher than the prices received by the farmers of any competing nation for the same products.

The Republican party has also aided the American farmer by relief of the sufferers in the drought-stricken areas, through loans for rehabilitation and through road building to provide employment, by the development of the inland waterway system, by the Perishable Product Act, by the strengthening of the extension system, and by the appropriation of $125,000,000 to recapitalize the Federal Loan Banks and enable them to extend time to worthy borrowers.

The Republican party pledges itself to the principle of assistance to cooperative marketing associations, owned and controlled by the farmers themselves, through the provisions of the Agricultural Marketing Act, which will be promptly amended or modified as experience shows to be necessary to accomplish the objects set forth in the preamble of that act.

The American farmer is entitled not only to tariff schedules on his products but to protection from substitutes therefor.

The party pledges itself to make such revision of tariff schedules as economic changes require to maintain the parity of protection to agriculture with other industry.

We will support any plan which will help to balance production against demand, and thereby raise agricultural prices, provided it is economically sound, and administratively workable without burdensome bureaucracy.

The burden of taxation borne by the owners of farm land constitutes one of the major problems of agriculture. President Hoover has aptly and truly said—"Taxes upon real property are easiest to enforce and are the least flexible of all taxes. The tendency under pressure of need is to continue these taxes unchanged in times of depression, despite the decrease in the owner's income. Decreasing price and decreasing income results in an increasing burden upon property owners . . . which is now becoming almost unbearable. The tax burden upon real estate is wholly out of proportion to that upon other forms of property and income. There is no farm relief more needed to-day than tax relief."

The time has come for a reconsideration of our tax

systems, Federal, State and local, with a view to developing a better coordination, reducing duplication, and relieving unjust burdens. The Republican party pledges itself to this end.

More than all else, we point to the fact that, in the administration of executive departments, and in every plan of the President for the coordination of national effort and for strengthening our financial structure, for expanding credit, for rebuilding the rural credit system and laying the foundations for better prices, the President has insisted upon the interest of the American farmer.

The fundamental problem of American agriculture is the control of production to such volume as will balance supply with demand. In the solution of this problem the cooperative organization of farmers to plan production, and the tariff, to hold the home market for American farmers, are vital elements. A third element equally as vital is the control of the acreage of land under cultivation, as an aid to the efforts of the farmer to balance production.

We favor a national policy of land utilization which looks to national needs, such as the administration has already begun to formulate. Such a policy must foster reorganization of taxing units in areas beset by tax delinquency, and divert lands that are submarginal for crop production to other uses. The national welfare plainly can be served by the acquisition of submarginal lands for watershed protection, grazing, forestry, public parks, and game reserves. We favor such acquisitions.

The Tariff. The Republican party has always been the staunch supporter of the American system of a protective tariff. It believes that the home market, built up under that policy, the greatest and richest market in the world, belongs first to American agriculture, industry and labor. No pretext can justify the surrender of that market to such competition as would destroy our farms, mines and factories, and lower the standard of living which we have established for our workers.

Because many foreign countries have recently abandoned the gold standard, as a result of which the costs of many commodities produced in such countries have, at least for the time being, fallen materially in terms of

American currency, adequate tariff protection is today particularly essential to the welfare of the American people. The Tariff Commission should promptly investigate individual commodities so affected by currency depreciation, and report to the President any increase in duties found necessary to equalize domestic with foreign costs of production.

To fix the duties on some thousands of commodities, subject to highly complex conditions, is necessarily a difficult technical task. It is unavoidable that some of the rates established by legislation should, even at the time of their enactment, be too low or too high. Moreover, a subsequent change in costs or other conditions may render obsolete a rate that was before appropriate. The Republican party has, therefore, long supported the policy of a flexible tariff, giving power to the President, after investigation by an impartial commission and in accordance with prescribed principles, to modify the rates named by the Congress.

We commend the President's veto of the measure, sponsored by Democratic Congressmen, which would have transferred from the President to the Congress the authority to put into effect the findings of the Tariff Commission. Approval of the measure would have returned tariff making to politics and destroyed the progress made during ten years of effort to lift it out of log-rolling methods. We pledge the Republican party to a policy which will retain the gains made and enlarge the present scope of greater progress.

We favor the extension of the general Republican principle of tariff protection to our natural resource industries, including the products of our farms, forests, mines and oil wells, with compensatory duties on the manufactured and refined products thereof.

Veterans. Our country is honored whenever it bestows relief on those who have faithfully served its flag. The Republican party, appreciative of this solemn obligation and honor, has made its sentiments evident in Congress.

Increased hospital facilities have been provided, payments in compensation have more than doubled, and in the matter of rehabilitations, pensions, and insurance, generous provision has been made. The administration of laws dealing with the relief of veterans and their dependents has been a difficult task, but every effort has been made to carry service to the veteran and bring about not only a better and generous interpretation of the law, but a sympathetic consideration of the many problems of the veteran.

We believe that every veteran incapacitated in any degree by reason of illness or injuries attributable to service in defense of his country should be cared for and compensated, so far as compensation is possible, by a grateful nation, and that the dependents of those who lost their lives in war or whose death since the war in which service was rendered is traceable to service causes, should be provided for adequately. Legislation should be in accord with this principle.

Disability from causes subsequent and not attributable to war and the support of dependents of deceased veterans whose death is unconnected with war, have been to some measure accepted obligations of the nation as a part of the debt due.

A careful study should be made of existing veterans legislation with a view to eliminating inequalities and injustices and effecting all possible economies, but without departing from our purpose to provide on a sound basis full and adequate relief for our service-disabled men, their widows and orphans.

Foreign Affairs. Our relations with foreign nations have been carried on by President Hoover with consistency and firmness but with mutual understanding and peace with all nations. The world has been overwhelmed with economic strain which has provoked extreme nationalism in every quarter, has overturned many governments, stirred the springs of suspicion and distrust, and tried the spirit of international cooperation, but we have held to our own course steadily and successfully. The party will continue to maintain its attitude of protecting our national interests and policies wherever threatened, but at the same time promoting common understanding of the varying needs and aspirations of other nations and going forward in harmony with other peoples without alliances or foreign partnerships. The facilitation of world intercourse, the freeing of commerce from unnecessary impediments, the settlement of international difficulties by conciliation and the methods of law, and the elimination of war as a resort of national policy have been and will be our party program.

Friendship and Commerce. We believe in and look forward to the steady enlargement of the principles of equality of treatment between nations great and small, the concession of sovereignty and self-administration to every nation which is capable of carrying on stable government and conducting sound and orderly relationships with other peoples, and the cultivation of trade and intercourse on the basis of uniformity of opportunity of all nations.

In pursuance of these principles, which have steadily gained favor in the world, the administration has asked no special favors in commerce, has protested discriminations whenever they arose, and has steadily cemented this procedure by reciprocal treaties guaranteeing equality for trade and residence. The historic American policy known as the "most favored nation principle" has been our guiding program and we believe that policy to be the only one consistent with a full development of international trade, the only one suitable for a country having as wide and diverse a commerce as America and the one most appropriate for us in view of the great variety of our industrial, agricultural and mineral products and the traditions of our people. Any other plan involves bargains and partnerships with foreign nations and as a permanent policy is unsuited to America's position.

Conditions on the Pacific. Events in the Far East, involving the employment of arms on a large scale in a controversy between Japan and China, have caused world-wide concern in the past year and sorely tried the bulwarks erected to insure peace and pacific means for the settlement of international disputes. The controversy has not only threatened the security of the nations bordering the Pacific, but has challenged the maintenance of the policy of the Open Door in China and the administrative and political integrity of that people, programs which upon American initiation were adopted more than a generation ago and secured by international treaty. The President and his Secretary of State have maintained throughout the controversy a just balance between Japan and China, taking always a firm position to avoid entanglement in the dispute but consistently upholding the established international policies and the treaty rights and interests of the United States, and never condoning developments that endangered the obligation of treaties or the peace of the world. Throughout the controversy our government has acted in harmony with the governments represented in the League of Nations, always making it clear that American policy would be determined at home but always lending a hand in the common interest of peace and order.

In the application of the principles of the Kellogg Pact the American Government has taken the lead, following the principle that a breach of the pact or a threat of infringement thereof was a matter of international concern wherever and however brought about.

As a further step the Secretary of State, upon the instruction of the President, adopted the principle later enlarged upon in his letter to the Chairman of the Committee on Foreign Relations of the Senate that this government would not recognize any situation, treaty or agreement brought about between Japan and China by force and in defiance of the covenants of the Kellogg Pact. This principle, associated as it is with the name of President Hoover, was later adopted by the Assembly of the nations at Geneva as a rule for the conduct of all those governments. The principle remains to-day as an important contribution to international law and a significant moral and material barrier to prevent a nation obtaining the fruits of aggressive warfare. It thus opens a new pathway to peace and order.

We favor enactment by Congress of a measure that will authorize our government to call or participate in an international conference in case of any threat of nonfulfilment of Article 2 of the Treaty of Paris (Kellogg-Briand Pact).

Latin America. The policy of the administration has proved to our neighbors of Latin America that we have no imperialistic ambitions but that we wish only to promote the welfare and common interests of the independent nations in the Western Hemisphere. We have aided Nicaragua in the solution of its troubles and our marines are remaining in that country—in greatly reduced numbers—at the request of the Nicaraguan government, only to supervise the coming election. After that they will all be returned to the United States.

In Haiti, in accord with the recommendations of the Forbes Commission, appointed by the President, the various services of supervision are being rapidly withdrawn and only those will be retained which are mandatory under the treaties.

Throughout Latin America the policy of the Government of the United States has been and will, under Republican leadership, continue to be one of frank and friendly understanding.

World Court. The acceptance by America of membership in the World Court has been approved by three successive Republican Presidents and we commend this attitude of supporting in this form the settlement of international disputes by the rule of law. America should join its influence and gain a voice in this institution, which would offer us a safer, more judicial and expeditious instrument for the constantly recurring questions between us and other nations than is now available by arbitration.

Reduction of Armament. Conscious that the limitation of armament will contribute to security against war, and that the financial burdens of military preparation have been shamefully increased throughout the world, the administration under President Hoover has made steady efforts and marked progress in the direction of proportional reduction of arms by agreement with other nations. Upon his initiative a treaty between the chief naval powers at London in 1930, following the path marked by the Washington Conference of 1922, established a limitation of all types of fighting ships on a proportionate basis as between the three great naval powers. For the first time, a general limitation of a most costly branch of armament was successfully accomplished.

In the Geneva Disarmament Conference, now in progress, America is an active participant, and a representative delegation of our citizens is laboring for further progress in a cause to which this country has been an earnest contributor. This policy will be pursued.

Meanwhile, maintenance of our Navy on the basis of

parity with any nation is a fundamental policy to which the Republican party is committed. While in the interest of necessary government retrenchment, humanity and relief of the taxpayer we shall continue to exert our full influence upon the nations of the world in the cause of reduction of arms, we do not propose to reduce our navy defenses below that of any other nation.

National Defense. Armaments are relative and, therefore, flexible and subject to change as necessity demands. We believe that in time of war every material resource in the nation should bear its proportionate share of the burdens occasioned by the public need and that it is a duty of government to perfect plans in time of peace whereby this objective may be attained in war. We support the essential principles of the National Defense Act as amended in 1920 and by the Air Corps Act of 1926, and believe that the Army of the United States has through successive reductions, accomplished in the last twelve years, reached the irreducible minimum consistent with the self-reliance, self-respect and security of this country.

Labor and Immigration. We believe in the principle of high wages.

We favor the principle of the shorter work week and shorter work day with its application to government as well as to private employment, as rapidly and as constructively as conditions will warrant.

We favor legislation designed to stimulate, encourage and assist in the home building.

Immigration. The restriction of immigration is a Republican policy. Our party formulated and enacted into law the quota system which for the first time has made possible an adequate control of foreign immigration. Rigid examination of applicants in foreign countries has prevented the coming of criminals and other undesirable classes, while other provisions of the law have enabled the President to suspend immigration of foreign wage-earners, who otherwise, directly or indirectly, would have increased unemployment among native-born and legally resident foreign-born wage-earners in this country. As a result, immigration is now less than at any time during the past one hundred years.

We favor the continuance and strict enforcement of our present laws upon this subject.

Department of Labor. We commend the constructive work of the United States Department of Labor.

Labor. Collective bargaining by responsible representatives of employers and employees of their own choice without the interference of anyone is recognized and approved.

Legislation such as laws prohibiting alien contract labor, peonage labor, and the "Shanghai-ing" of sailors, the eight-hour labor law on government contracts, and in government employment; provision for railroad safety devices, of methods of conciliation, mediation and arbitration in industrial labor disputes, including the adjustment of railroad disputes, the providing of compensation for injury to government employees (the forerunner of Federal Workers' Compensation Act), and other laws to aid and protect labor are of Republican origin, and have had and will continue to have the unswerving support of the party.

Employment. We commend the constructive work of the United States Employment Service in the Department of Labor. This service was enlarged and its activities extended through an appropriation made possible by the President with the cooperation of the Congress. It has done high service for the unemployed in the ranks of civil life and in the ranks of the former soldiers of the World War.

Freedom of Speech. Freedom of speech, press and assemblage, are fundamental principles upon which our form of government rests. These vital principles should be preserved and protected.

Public Utilities. Supervision, regulation and control of interstate public utilities in the interest of the public is an established policy of the Republican party, to the credit of which stands the creation of the Interstate Commerce Commission with its authority to assure reasonable transportation rates, sound railway finance and adequate service.

As proof of the progress made by the Republican party in government control of public utilities, we cite the reorganization under this administration of the Federal

Power Commission with authority to administer the Federal Water Power Act. We urge legislation to authorize this commission to regulate the charges for electric current when transmitted across State lines.

Transportation. The promotion of agriculture, commerce and industry requires coordination of transportation by rail, highway, air and water. All should be subjected to appropriate and constructive regulation.

The public will of course select the form of transportation best fitted to its particular service, but the terms of competition fixed by public authority should operate without discrimination, so that all common carriers by rail, highway, air and water shall operate under conditions of equality.

The railroads constitute the backbone of our transportation system and perform an essential service for the country. The railroad industry is our largest employer of labor and the greatest consumer of goods. The restoration of their credit and the maintenance of their ability to render adequate service are of paramount importance to the public, to their many thousands of employees and to savings banks, insurance companies and other similar institutions, to which the savings of the people have been entrusted.

We should continue to encourage the further development of the merchant marine under American registry and ownership.

Under the present administration the American merchant fleet has been enlarged and strengthened until it now occupies second place among the merchant marines of the world.

By the gradual retirement of the government from the field of ship operations, and marked economies in costs, the United States Shipping Board will require no appropriation for the fiscal year 1933 for ship operations.

Saint Lawrence Seaway. The Republican party stands committed to the development of the Great Lakes-St. Lawrence Seaway. Under the direction of President Hoover negotiation of a treaty with Canada for this development is now at a favorable point. Recognizing the inestimable benefits which will accrue to the nation from placing the ports of the Great Lakes on an ocean base, the party reaffirms allegiance to this great project and pledges its best efforts to secure its early completion.

Inland Waterways. The Republican party recognizes that low cost transportation for bulk commodities will enable industry to develop in the midst of agriculture in the Mississippi Valley, thereby creating a home market for farm products in that section. With a view to aiding agriculture in the Middle West the present administration has pushed forward, as rapidly as possible, the improvement of the Mississippi Waterway System, and we favor a continued vigorous prosecution of these works to the end that agriculture and industry in that great area may enjoy the benefits of these improvements at the earliest possible date.

Highways. The Federal policy to cooperate with the States in the building of roads was thoroughly established when the Federal Highway Act of 1921 was adopted under a Republican Congress. Each year since that time appropriations have been made which have greatly increased the economic value of highway transportation and helped to raise the standards and opportunities of rural life.

We pledge our support to the continuation of this policy in accordance with our needs and resources.

Crime. We favor the enactment of rigid penal laws that will aid the States in stamping out the activities of gangsters, racketeers and kidnapers. We commend the intensive and effective drive made upon these public enemies by President Hoover and pledge our party to further efforts to the same purpose.

Narcotics. The Republican party pledges itself to continue the present relentless warfare against the illicit narcotic traffic and the spread of the curse of drug addiction among our people. This administration has by treaty greatly strengthened our power to deal with this traffic.

Civil Service. The merit system has been amply justified since the organization of the Civil Service by the Republican party. As a part of our governmental system it is now unassailable. We believe it should remain so.

The Eighteenth Amendment. The Republican party has always stood and stands to-day for obedience to and enforcement of the law as the very foundation of orderly government and civilization. There can be no national security otherwise. The duty of the President of the United States and of the officers of the law is clear. The law must be enforced as they find it enacted by the people. To these courses of action we pledge our nominees.

The Republican party is and always has been the party of the Constitution. Nullification by non-observance by individuals or State action threatens the stability of government.

While the Constitution makers sought a high degree of permanence, they foresaw the need of changes and provided for them. Article V limits the proposals of amendments to two methods: (1) Two-thirds of both Houses of Congress may propose amendments; or (2) On application of the legislatures of two-thirds of the States a national convention shall be called by Congress to propose amendments. Thereafter ratification must be had in one of two ways: (1) By the legislatures of three-fourths of the several States; or (2) By conventions held in three-fourths of the several States. Congress is given power to determine the mode of ratification.

Referendums without constitutional sanction cannot furnish a decisive answer. Those who propose them innocently are deluded by false hopes; those who propose them knowingly are deceiving the people.

A nation-wide controversy over the Eighteenth Amendment now distracts attention from the constructive solution of many pressing national problems. The principle of national prohibition as embodied in the Amendment was supported and opposed by members of both great political parties. It was submitted to the States by members of Congress of different political faith and ratified by State legislatures of different political majorities. It was not then and is now not a partisan political question.

Members of the Republican party hold different opinions with respect to it and no public official or member of the party should be pledged or forced to choose between his party affiliations and his honest convictions upon this question.

We do not favor a submission limited to the issue of retention or repeal. For the American nation never in its history has gone backward, and in this case the progress which has been thus far made must be preserved, while the evils must be eliminated.

We, therefore, believe that the people should have an opportunity to pass upon a proposed amendment the provision of which, while retaining in the Federal government power to preserve the gains already made in dealing with the evils inherent in the liquor traffic, shall allow States to deal with the problem as their citizens may determine, but subject always to the power of the Federal government to protect those States where prohibition may exist and safeguard our citizens everywhere from the return of the saloon and attendant abuses.

Such an amendment should be promptly submitted to the States by Congress, to be acted upon by State conventions called for that sole purpose in accordance with the provisions of Article V of the Constitution, and adequately safeguarded so as to be truly representative.

Conservation. The wise use of all natural resources freed from monopolistic control is a Republican policy, initiated by Theodore Roosevelt. The Roosevelt, Coolidge and Hoover reclamation projects bear witness to the continuation of that policy. Forestry and all other conservation activities have been supported and enlarged.

The conservation of oil is a major problem to the industry and the nation. The administration has sought to bring coordination of effort through the States, the producers and the Federal government. Progress has been made and the effort will continue.

Negro. For seventy years the Republican party has been the friend of the American Negro. Vindication of the right of the Negro citizen to enjoy the full benefits of life, liberty, and the pursuit of happiness is traditional in the Republican party, and our party stands pledged to maintain equal opportunity and rights for our Negro citizens. We do not propose to depart from that tradition nor to alter the spirit or letter of that pledge.

Hawaii. We believe that the existing status of self-government which for many years has been enjoyed by the citizens of the Territory of Hawaii should be maintained, and that officials appointed to administer the government should be bona-fide residents of the Territory.

Puerto Rico. Puerto Rico being a part of the United States and its inhabitants American citizens, we believe that they are entitled to a good-faith recognition of the spirit and purposes of their Organic Act. We, therefore, favor the inclusion of the Island in all legislative and administrative measures enacted or adopted by Congress or otherwise for the economic benefit of their fellow citizens of the mainland.

We also believe that in so far as possible all officials appointed to administer the affairs of the Island government should be qualified by at least five years of bona-fide residence therein.

Alaska. We favor the policy of giving to the people of Alaska the widest possible territorial self-government and the selection so far as possible of bona-fide residents for positions in that Territory and the placing of its citizens on an equality with those in the several States.

Welfare Work and Children. The children of our nation, our future citizens, have had the most solicitous thought of our President. Child welfare and protection has been a major effort of this administration. The organization of the White House Conference on Child Health and Protection is regarded as one of the outstanding accomplishments of this administration.

Welfare work in all its phases has had the support of the President and aid of the administration. The work of organized agencies, local, State and Federal, has been advanced and an increased impetus given by that recognition and help. We approve and pledge a continuation of that policy.

Indians. We favor the fullest protection of the property rights of the American Indians and the provision for them of adequate educational and health facilities.

Reorganization of Government Bureaus. Efficiency and economy demand reorganization of government bureaus. The problem is non-partisan and must be so treated if it is to be solved. As a result of years of study and personal contact with conflicting activities and wasteful duplication of effort, the President is particularly fitted to direct measures to correct the situation. We favor legislation by Congress which will give him the required authority.

Democratic Failure. The vagaries of the present Democratic House of Representatives offer characteristic and appalling proof of the existing incapacity of that party for leadership in a national crisis. Individualism running amuck has displaced party discipline and has trampled underfoot party leadership. A bewildered electorate has viewed the spectacle with profound dismay and deep misgivings. Goaded to desperation by their confessed failure, the party leaders have resorted to "pork barrel" legislation to obtain a unity of action which could not otherwise be achieved. A Republican President stands resolutely between the helpless citizen and the disasters threatened by such measures; and the people, regardless of party, will demand his continued service. Many times during his useful life has Herbert Hoover responded to such a call, and his response has never disappointed. He will not disappoint us now.

Party Government. The delays and differences which recently hampered efforts to obtain legislation imperatively demanded by prevailing critical conditions strikingly illustrate the menace to self-government brought about by the weakening of party ties and party fealty. Experience has demonstrated that coherent political parties are indispensable agencies for the prompt and effective operation of the functions of our government under the Constitution. Only by united party action can consistent, well planned and wholesome legislative programs be enacted. We believe that the majority of the Congressmen elected in the name of a party have the right and duty to determine the general policies of that party requiring Congressional action, and that Congressmen belonging to that party are in general, bound to adhere to such policies. Any other course inevitably makes of Congress a body of detached delegates which, instead of representing the collective wisdom of our people, become the confused voices of a heterogeneous group of unrelated local prejudices. We believe that the time has come when Senators and Representatives of the United States should be impressed with the inflexible truth that their first concern should be the welfare of the United States and the well-being of all of its people, and that stubborn pride of individual opinion is not a virtue but an obstacle to the orderly and successful achievement of the objects of representative government. Only by cooperation can self-government succeed. Without it, election under a party aegis becomes a false pretense. We earnestly request that Republicans through the Union demand that their representatives in the Congress pledge themselves to these principles, to the end that the insidious influences of party disintegration may not undermine the very foundations of the Republic.

Conclusion. In contrast with the Republican policies and record, we contrast those of the Democratic as evidenced by the action of the House of Representatives under Democratic leadership and control, which includes:

1. The issuance of fiat currency;
2. Instructions to the Federal Reserve Board and the Secretary of the Treasury to attempt to manipulate commodity prices;
3. The guarantee of bank deposits;
4. The squandering of the public resources and the unbalancing of the budget through pork-barrel appropriations which bear little relation to distress and would tend through delayed business revival to decrease rather than increase employment;

Generally on economic matters we pledge the Republican party—

1. To maintain unimpaired the national credit.
2. To defend and preserve a sound currency and an honest dollar.
3. To stand steadfastly by the principle of a balanced budget.
4. To devote ourselves fearlessly and unremittingly to the task of eliminating abuses and extravagance and of drastically cutting the cost of government so as to reduce the heavy burden of taxation.
5. To use all available means consistent with sound financial and economic principles to promote an expansion of credit, to stimulate business and relieve unemployment.
6. To a thorough study of the conditions which per-

mitted the credit and the credit machinery of the country to be made available without adequate check for wholesale speculation in securities, resulting in ruinous consequences to millions of our citizens and to the national economy, and to correct those conditions so that they shall not recur.

Recognizing that real relief to unemployment must come through a revival of industrial activity and agriculture, to the promotion of which our every effort must be directed, our party in State and Nation undertakes to do all in its power that is humanly possible to see that distress is fully relieved in accordance with American principles and traditions.

No successful solution of the problems before the country to-day can be expected from a Congress and a President separated by partisan lines, or opposed in purposes and principles. Responsibility cannot be placed unless a clear mandate is given by returning to Washington a Congress and a Chief Executive united in principles and program. The return to power of the Republican party with that mandate is the duty of every voter who believes in the doctrines of the party and its program as herein stated. Nothing less, we believe, will insure the orderly recovery of the country and that return to prosperous days which every American so ardently desires.

The Republican party faces the future unafraid!

With courage and confidence in ultimate success, we will strive against the forces that strike at our social and economic ideals, our political institutions.

THE DEMOCRATIC PARTY PLATFORM, 1932

In this time of unprecedented economic and social distress the Democratic party declares its conviction that the chief causes of this condition were the disastrous policies pursued by our government since the World War, of economic isolation, fostering the merger of competitive businesses into monopolies and encouraging the indefensible expansion and contraction of credit for private profit at the expense of the public.

Those who were responsible for these policies have abandoned the ideals on which the war was won and thrown away the fruits of victory, thus rejecting the greatest opportunity in history to bring peace, prosperity, and happiness to our people and to the world.

They have ruined our foreign trade; destroyed the values of our commodities and products, crippled our banking system, robbed millions of our people of their life savings, and thrown millions more out of work, produced wide-spread poverty and brought the government to a state of financial distress unprecedented in time of peace.

The only hope for improving present conditions, restoring employment, affording permanent relief to the people and bringing the nation back to the proud position of domestic happiness and of financial, industrial, agricultural and commercial leadership in the world lies in a drastic change in economic government policies.

We believe that a party platform is a covenant with the people to be faithfully kept by the party when entrusted with power, and that the people are entitled to know in plain words the terms of the contract to which they are asked to subscribe. We hereby declare this to be the platform of the Democratic party:

The Democratic party solemnly promises by appropriate action to put into effect the principles, policies, and reforms herein advocated, and to eradicate the policies, methods, and practices herein condemned. We advocate an immediate and drastic reduction of governmental expenditures by abolishing useless commissions and offices, consolidating departments and bureaus, and eliminating extravagance, to accomplish a saving of not less than twenty-five per cent in the cost of Federal government, and we call upon the Democratic party in the States to make a zealous effort to achieve a proportionate result.

We favor maintenance of the national credit by a Federal budget annually balanced on the basis of accurate executive estimates within revenues, raised by a system of taxation levied on the principle of ability to pay.

We advocate a sound currency to be preserved at all hazards and an international monetary conference called on the invitation of our government to consider the rehabilitation of silver and related questions.

We advocate a competitive tariff for revenue, with a fact-finding tariff commission free from executive interference, reciprocal tariff agreements with other nations, and an international economic conference designed to restore international trade and facilitate exchange.

We advocate the extension of Federal credit to the States to provide unemployment relief wherever the diminishing resources of the States makes it impossible for them to provide for the needy; expansion of the Federal program of necessary and useful construction affected with a public interest, such as adequate flood control and waterways.

We advocate the spread of employment by a substantial reduction in the hours of labor, the encouragement of the shorter week by applying that principle in government service. We advocate advance planning of public works.

We advocate unemployment and old-age insurance under State laws.

We favor the restoration of agriculture, the nation's basic industry; better financing of farm mortgages through recognized farm bank agencies at low rates of interest on an amortization plan, giving preference to credits for the redemption of farms and homes sold under foreclosure.

Extension and development of the farm cooperative movement and effective control of crop surpluses so that our farmers may have the full benefit of the domestic market.

The enactment of every constitutional measure that will aid the farmers to receive for their basic farm commodities prices in excess of cost.

We advocate a Navy and an Army adequate for national defense, based on a survey of all facts affecting the existing establishments, that the people in time of peace may not be burdened by an expenditure fast approaching a billion dollars annually.

We advocate strengthening and impartial enforcement of the anti-trust laws, to prevent monopoly and unfair trade practices, and revision thereof for the better protection of labor and the small producer and distributor.

The conservation, development, and use of the nation's water power in the public interest.

The removal of government from all fields of private

enterprise except where necessary to develop public works and natural resources in the common interest.

We advocate protection of the investing public by requiring to be filed with the government and carried in advertisements of all offerings of foreign and domestic stocks and bonds true information as to bonuses, commissions, principal invested, and interests of the sellers.

Regulation to the full extent of Federal power of:

(a) Holding companies which sell securities in interstate commerce;

(b) Rates of utility companies operating across State lines;

(c) Exchanges in securities and commodities.

We advocate quicker methods of realizing on assets for the relief of depositors of suspended banks, and a more rigid supervision of national banks for the protection of depositors and the prevention of the use of their moneys in speculation to the detriment of local credits.

The severance of affiliated security companies from, and the divorce of the investment banking business from, commercial banks, and further restriction of Federal Reserve banks in permitting the use of Federal Reserve facilities for speculative purposes.

We advocate the full measure of justice and generosity for all war veterans who have suffered disability or disease caused by or resulting from actual service in time of war and for their dependents.

We advocate a firm foreign policy, including peace with all the world and the settlement of international disputes by arbitration; no interference in the internal affairs of other nations; the sanctity of treaties and the maintenance of good faith and of good will in financial obligations; adherence to the World Court with appending reservations; the Pact of Paris abolishing war as an instrument of national policy, to be made effective by provisions for consultation and conference in case of threatened violations of treaties.

International agreements for reduction of armaments and cooperation with nations of the Western Hemisphere to maintain the spirit of the Monroe Doctrine.

We oppose cancelation of the debts owing to the United States by foreign nations.

We advocate independence for the Philippines; ultimate statehood for Puerto Rico;

The employment of American citizens in the operation of the Panama Canal;

Simplification of legal procedure and reorganization of the judicial system to make the attainment of justice speedy, certain, and at less cost;

Continuous publicity of political contributions and expenditures; strengthening of the Corrupt Practices Act and severe penalties for misappropriation of campaign funds.

We advocate the repeal of the Eighteenth Amendment. To effect such repeal we demand that the Congress immediately propose a Constitutional Amendment to truly representative conventions in the States called to act solely on that proposal; we urge the enactment of such measures by the several States as will actually promote temperance, effectively prevent the return of the saloon and bring the liquor traffic into the open under complete supervision and control by the States.

We demand that the Federal government effectively exercise its power to enable the States to protect themselves against importation of intoxicating liquors in violation of their laws.

Pending repeal, we favor immediate modification of the Volstead Act to legalize the manufacture and sale of beer and other beverages of such alcoholic content as is permissible under the Constitution and to provide therefrom a proper and needed revenue.

We advocate continuous responsibility of government for human welfare, especially for the protection of children.

We condemn the improper and excessive use of money in political activities.

We condemn paid lobbies of special interests to influence members of Congress and other public servants by personal contact.

We condemn action and utterances of high public officials designed to influence stock-exchange prices.

We condemn the open and covert resistance of administration officials to every effort made by Congressional committees to curtail the extravagant expenditures of the government and to revoke improvident subsidies granted to favorite interests.

We condemn the extravagance of the Farm Board, its disastrous action, which made the government a speculator of farm products, and the unsound policy of restricting agricultural products to the demands of domestic markets.

We condemn the usurpation of power by the State Department in assuming to pass upon foreign securities offered by international bankers, as a result of which billions of dollars in questionable bonds have been sold to the public upon the implied approval of the Federal government.

We condemn the Hawley-Smoot Tariff Law, the prohibitive rates of which have resulted in retaliatory action by more than forty countries, created international economic hostilities, destroyed international trade, driven our factories into foreign countries, robbed the American farmer of his foreign markets, and increased the cost of production.

In conclusion, to accomplish these purposes and to recover economic liberty we pledge the nominees of this convention the best efforts of a great party whose founder announced the doctrine which guides us now in the hour of our country's need:

Equal rights to all; special privileges to none.

— 3 —

CONGRESS

DEBATE ON SENATE RULES CHANGE, 1959 *

Foreign observers have often remarked that in the United States political issues tend to become dissolved in constitutional questions. The debate on the proposed Senate rules changes illustrates this point.

Senators seeking to enact civil rights legislation believed that on several occasions their efforts had been thwarted by southern filibusters or threats of filibuster. Consequently, they attempted to alter the rules of the Senate to permit debates to be terminated more easily by motion of cloture. Senate majority leader Lyndon B. Johnson countered with a more moderate proposal. The discussion soon devolved into an argument over the nature of the Senate and its position in the American system of government. Excerpts from that debate are reprinted below.

Mr. JOHNSON of Texas. Mr. President, I suggest the absence of a quorum.

The VICE PRESIDENT. The Secretary will call the roll.

The Chief Clerk proceeded to call the roll.

Mr. JOHNSON of Texas. Mr. President, I ask unanimous consent that the order for the quorum call be rescinded.

The VICE PRESIDENT. Without objection, it is so ordered.

* *Congressional Record,* January 8-12, 1959, pp. 63-476.

Mr. MONRONEY. Mr. President, will the Senator from Texas yield time to me?

Mr. JOHNSON of Texas. I yield to the Senator from Oklahoma.

Mr. MONRONEY. Mr. President, I strongly urge the Members of the Senate to support the motion of the majority leader to proceed to the immediate consideration of the resolution to amend rule XXII.

Mr. JOHNSON of Texas. Mr. President, may we have order?

The VICE PRESIDENT. The Senate will be in order.

Mr. MONRONEY. Mr. President, I urge such support regardless of any Senator's individual views on the specific amendment of rule XXII which is proposed in the resolution.

If the resolution is made the pending business of the Senate, each Senator will be assured an opportunity to propose whatever alternative he wishes, and to have the Senate express its approval or disapproval of such alternative by majority vote. We are assured, by the adoption of this motion, of an immediate opportunity to vote on a more strict rule of cloture.

This has been the objective which some Members have sought to reach by another means, namely, by a motion that the Senate proceed to adopt rules.

I suggest to those Senators who have supported such a motion in the past and those who were prepared to support it at the beginning of this Congress, that this objective—an opportunity to adopt a new cloture rule by majority vote—is achieved just as surely by the adoption of the motion of the majority leader that the Senate proceed to consider amendment of rule XXII. . . .

Mr. MANSFIELD. I should like to ask the Senator from Oklahoma to yield to me for the purpose of propounding a number of parliamentary inquiries.

Mr. MONRONEY. I yield.

Mr. MANSFIELD. With the understanding, of course, that the Senator from Oklahoma does not lose the floor.

Mr. MONRONEY. I yield with that understanding . . .

Mr. MANSFIELD. . . . What I am trying to have made clear is this: There has been talk of hijacking and blackjacking because the majority leader, by reason of his position, was recognized first yesterday and submitted a resolution. As I understand the rulings of the Chair, every Member of the Senate will have a chance to vote yea or nay on the Anderson proposal, on the Douglas proposal, and on the Johnson of Texas proposal. Is not that correct?

The VICE PRESIDENT. The Senator from Montana is correct. . . .

Mr. LAUSCHE. Mr. President, will the Senator from Oklahoma yield?

Mr. MONRONEY. I am happy to yield.

Mr. LAUSCHE. Having in mind the answers given by the Chair to the Senator from Montana to the effect that the Senate will have the right to pass its judgment on each of the issues raised, I now ask this question: By what number of votes would a measure be carried if the procedure described by the Senator from Montana were carried out? Would it be by a majority vote or a two-thirds vote?

The VICE PRESIDENT. If the Chair correctly understands the question of the Senator from Ohio, the adoption of a motion to lay aside the resolution of the Senator from Texas or the adoption of an amendment to the rules would be by majority vote.

Mr. LAUSCHE. Let us assume that the proposal of the four Senators previously mentioned came before the Senate. Would that proposal have to be carried by a majority vote of the Senators voting, or would its adoption require a two-thirds vote?

The VICE PRESIDENT. It would require a majority vote. . . .

Mr. RUSSELL, Mr. JAVITS, and other Senators addressed the Chair.

The VICE PRESIDENT. Does the Senator from Oklahoma yield; and, if so, to whom?

Mr. MONRONEY. I yield first to the Senator from Georgia, under the conditions previously stated.

Mr. RUSSELL. Mr. President, I desire to propound a parliamentary inquiry. The Chair has stated on several occasions, and has reiterated this morning, that he is of the opinion that most of the rules of the Senate are applicable here today, and therefore are continuing. There are other rules, to which the Chair referred by rule and by number, as to which the Chair is of the opinion that they are not applicable, for the reason the Chair has stated—namely, that he thinks they are unconstitutional.

I should like to ask the Chair on what rule or what statute or what provision of the Constitution of the United States the Chair, as Presiding Officer of the Senate, relies for this attempt to exercise the right to select which rules of the Senate are applicable and which are not applicable, and which are constitutional and which are unconstitutional.

The VICE PRESIDENT. The Chair is bound by the rules of the Senate, as adopted by the Senate. The Chair also has a constitutional responsibility. The Chair has indicated on several occasions, moreover, that while it is the opinion of the Chair that the Senate rules, in the respects to which the Chair has referred, are not in accordance with constitutional mandate, it is only the Chair's opinion, and that question, if it is raised, will be submitted to the Senate itself for its decision.

Mr. RUSSELL. Does the Chair arrive at that conclusion of his right to render these advisory opinions under his constitutional position as a member of the executive branch of the Government, or in his status as Presiding Officer of the Senate?

The VICE PRESIDENT. The Chair renders that opinion in his status as Presiding Officer of the Senate. The Chair should point out he renders this opinion only in response to parliamentary inquiries which have been propounded by various Members of the Senate.

Mr. RUSSELL. They have been very freely propounded, and the Chair has freely answered; but can the Chair point to any precedent where any Presiding Officer of the Senate has sought to rule that any rule of the Senate is unconstitutional? . . .

The VICE PRESIDENT. The Chair has no precedent at hand, but the Chair points out that it is very common for Presiding Officers to indicate their opinions with regard to the rules of the Senate and other matters. If there is any doubt about it, the Chair suggests that Members of the Senate read the various briefs presented to the Presiding Officer on this question.

Mr. RUSSELL. I have labored through a brief which was submitted to the Chair, but I found in the brief nothing which, in my opinion, would give the Chair the right to declare a rule of the Senate unconstitutional. Of course, the Chair has a right to construe the rules and apply them; but to strike one down by an advisory opinion is, in my opinion, something new.

The VICE PRESIDENT. If the Senator will allow the Chair to state his position correctly, the Chair has not been so presumptuous as to strike down a rule of the Senate. The Chair has been careful to state that he was expressing his opinion only as to constitutionality . . .

Mr. JOHNSON of Texas. I ask the Chair to lay before the Senate Resolution 5.

Mr. DOUGLAS. Mr. President, who has the floor?

The VICE PRESIDENT. The Chair lays before the Senate——

Mr. DOUGLAS. Mr. President, a point of order.

The VICE PRESIDENT laid before the Senate Senate Resolution 5, which was read by the legislative clerk, as follows:

Resolved, That subsection 2 of rule XXII of the Standing Rules of the Senate is amended (1) by striking out "except subsection 3 of rule XXII," and (2) by striking out "two-thirds of the Senators duly chosen and sworn" and inserting in lieu thereof "two-thirds of the Senators present and voting."

SEC. 2. Subsection 3 of rule XXII of the Standing Rules of the Senate is amended by striking out "and of subsection 2 of this rule."

SEC. 3. Rule XXXII of the Standing Rules of the Senate is amended by inserting "1." immediately preceding "At", and by adding at the end thereof a new paragraph as follows:

"2. The rules of the Senate shall continue from one Congress to the next Congress unless they are changed as provided in these rules." . . .

Mr. JOHNSON of Texas. Mr. President, I ask the

Senator from Oklahoma if he will permit me to make a brief statement.

Mr. MONRONEY. I yield, and ask unanimous consent that I may be permitted to resume my remarks following the statement of the majority leader.

The VICE PRESIDENT. Is there objection? The Chair hears none and the Senator from Texas may proceed.

Mr. JOHNSON of Texas. Mr. President, I should like to say that with respect to the motion proposed by the Senator from New Mexico [Mr. ANDERSON] yesterday, or with respect to any motion he may intend to propose today, which involves submitting to the Senate the question of whether it wants to displace the Johnson resolution and go into the question of an entire new set of rules, I will be glad to ask unanimous consent that it be in order to consider that motion today, without having it lie over a day under rule XL . . .

The VICE PRESIDENT. Is there objection to the Senator from New Mexico submitting his motion? . . .

Mr. ANDERSON. Mr. President, I submit the motion.

The VICE PRESIDENT. Without objection, the clerk will read the motion.

The CHIEF CLERK. Mr. ANDERSON moves "that the Senate, in accordance with article I, section 5 of the Constitution which declares that 'each House may determine the rules of its proceedings' now proceed to the immediate consideration of the adoption of rules for the Senate of the 86th Congress."

The VICE PRESIDENT. Will the Senator now state his unanimous-consent request? . . .

Mr. JOHNSON of Texas. Very well. I ask unanimous consent that, notwithstanding the provisions of rule XL, it may be in order to consider this motion as a substitute for the Johnson resolution. If adopted, of course, it would displace the Johnson resolution and prolong debate even further, in my opinion.

The VICE PRESIDENT. Is there objection to the unanimous-consent request of the Senator from Texas? Without objection, the unanimous-consent request is agreed to. . . .

Mr. ANDERSON. Mr. President, my interest in the proposal to adopt rules at the beginning of the session is based upon enough experience to know that if we do not act on the rules now, we will never have opportunity to act during this session. We have been discussing this situation through a number of sessions of Congress. . . .

[*Anderson then described several previous unsuccessful attempts to amend the Senate rules in the manner he desired.*]

Mr. LONG. Mr. President, will the Senator yield?

Mr. ANDERSON. I yield to the Senator from Louisiana.

Mr. LONG. Reference has been made to the book I hold in my hand. It has been called the rulebook. Of course, it is the "Senate Manual," which contains the rules of the Senate. It contains some rules written by Thomas Jefferson, in "Jefferson's Manual." We have followed some of the precedents in "Jefferson's Manual." Thomas Jefferson has not been here for 150 years. Do my colleagues wish with regard to Thomas Jefferson and with respect to the rest of the rules to do the same thing that is proposed?

The book also contains the "Declaration of Independence." Do the Senators wish to throw that out, too, now that Thomas Jefferson is gone?

I see in the book also the Constitution, which was written by men who have not been here for 150 years. Do Senators wish to do away with those portions of the "Manual"?

Mr. PASTORE. Mr. President, will the Senator yield so that I may propound a question?

Mr. ANDERSON. I yield.

Mr. PASTORE. I should like to ask the Senator from Louisiana, For what rules of the Senate did Thomas Jefferson vote?

Mr. LONG. I did not hear the question.

Mr. PASTORE. For what rules of the Senate did Thomas Jefferson vote, that we are violating now? We are talking about the right of the Senate to make its own rules. If we do not have rules, we can vote for the parliamentary rules which have been prescribed by Thomas Jefferson, or we can adopt "Robert's Rules of Order." That may be so. All I am saying is that fundamentally, under the Constitution, it has been decided that the Senate can make its own rules. But which Senate? The Senate of 1800 or the Senate of 1959? I say that if the Senate of 1959 has the responsibility to do the people's business, it ought to have the responsibility of adopting its own rules.

Mr. LONG. That is what we are trying to do. We are attempting to change some of our rules. Our rules include precedents which have been handed down to us. Those precedents oftentimes are binding on the Senate. They have been adopted together with the rules.

If we look at "Jefferson's Manual," we find that the rules do not provide for certain things in certain circumstances.

Mr. ANDERSON. I was just about to quote Thomas Jefferson. He said:

"Can one generation bind another, and all others, in succession forever?

"I think not. The Creator has made the earth for the living, not the dead."

In the Senate of the United States, I say to the Senator from Louisiana, we ought to write rules for the living, not the dead. New Senators come to this body, and there is no reason why those new Senators should be told that they are Senators in every respect except in the right to make rules. They should not be told, "You are vassals when it comes to writing rules. The Senators who were present in 1949 have said how you should live here. You have not a word to say for yourselves about how you shall live." . . .

Mr. O'MAHONEY. Mr. President, will the Senator yield?

Mr. ANDERSON. I yield.

Mr. O'MAHONEY. I have listened to the interrogations and the answers which have been given, and I should like to ask the Senator from New Mexico another question. Will he be so kind as to tell me why the adoption of the Johnson resolution would deprive the Senate of any power to change rules by a majority vote?

Mr. ANDERSON. The Johnson resolution contains section 3, which provides a new section 2, and that section 2 will read:

The rules of the Senate shall continue from one Congress to the next Congress unless they are changed as provided in these rules.

Mr. O'MAHONEY. Are not the rules of the Senate as they now exist, with the exception of rule XXII, against which I shall vote, amply sufficient to allow the Senate to change its rules by majority vote at any time?

Mr. ANDERSON. No. I think the ruling has been made, round after round, that it requires a sizable vote—no; not a sizable vote, but a majority vote, to get the question before the Senate.

Mr. O'MAHONEY. But the Johnson amendment strikes out that provision.

Mr. ANDERSON. It would still require a two-thirds vote to impose cloture.

Mr. O'MAHONEY. I beg the Senator's pardon. That provision is stricken out by the Johnson amendment, so that it cannot continue from generation to generation or from Congress to Congress if the amendment is adopted.

Mr. ANDERSON. I am sorry, but that still does not happen to be the case, in my opinion. This provision says that the rules are to continue in effect unless they are changed.

In the succeeding Congress, the one which will begin in 1961, the able Senator from Wisconsin [Mr. PROXMIRE] might rise and say, "I move that the rules of the Senate be changed in the following particulars." He must be able to enforce cloture to secure consideration of his motion. He must obtain a two-thirds vote of the Senate to reach that point. . . .

Mr. DOUGLAS. Mr. President, . . . I shall try to speak briefly, but I shall try to make clear why we believed the Anderson motion is essential. . . .

Underneath all the verbiage, underneath all the parliamentary maneuvers . . . we are trying to establish at the very beginning of the Senate the right of the Senate, by a majority vote, to adopt rules, and not to be governed by the straitjacket which was imposed in 1949.

Section 2 of the rule XXII is bad enough. It provides that cloture or limitation of debate on a bill can be carried through only by a two-thirds vote of the entire membership of the Senate. That really imprisoned a number of bills, including those relating to civil rights, in a cell very difficult for the public to locate, or even to unlock . . .

But the third section of rule XXII threw away the key

. . . because it provided that even though a large group in the Senate—even though two-thirds, three-fourths, three-fifths, or five-sixths—were determined to change the rules, they could not do so because unanimous consent was needed to change the rules. . . .

The adoption of the Anderson motion . . . will establish the basic principle that a majority of the Senate in a new Congress can adopt or amend Senate rules for that new Senate, free from the restrictions of the old rules, which in effect rigidly limit that rule-making power. . . .

I regret that my good friend from Georgia used the expression this afternoon that the Senate consisted of ambassadors from their sovereign States. That, perhaps, was the interpretation, under the Articles of Confederation, and the Delegates to the Continental Congress I think, perhaps, primarily regarded themselves as such.

But we are a United States now—and have been a United States for at least 93 years. I regret to see the pre-1860 language used upon the floor of the Senate at the present time. We are not merely Senators from Minnesota, Pennsylvania, Illinois, Alaska, Ohio, Michigan, Utah, North Carolina, Florida, Louisiana, Georgia, Alabama, and South Carolina; we are also Senators of the United States of America. It is about time that fact is realized.

My friend, Carl Sandburg, says that the war of 1861 to 1865 was fought on the question of grammar; whether the proper phrase should be "the United States are" or "the United States is"; whether we are a mere federation of sovereign States or whether we are a nation.

I am not here to wave the bloody shirt or to refight that war. I will merely say that since 1865, at least, the United States is a nation—is a nation. There perhaps are some people who do not realize this fact now, but I want to predict that they are going to realize it. The United States is a nation, and we meet in one House of that Nation, representing our State interests, it is true, but also representing our national interests, and the national interests should be controlling and predominant.

What bearing does that have on this dispute? It has this bearing: that the Senate is not an assembly of the United Nations. Neither is it a Security Council of the United Nations. No one in this body should have the power of the veto. No small groups should have the power of the veto.

The Constitution provides that the majority will is to prevail except in those matters which are specifically stated to the contrary, and there are only five such. The Constitution states that amendments to the Constitution must be submitted by a two-thirds vote of both Houses; that treaties must be ratified by a two-thirds vote of the Senate; that impeachment requires a two-thirds vote; that expulsion of a Member requires a two-thirds vote; and that to override a veto a two-thirds vote is required.

But on every other subject a majority is supposed to prevail, in default of specific language to the contrary. There is no such language about House rules or Senate rules. There is no such provision in the Constitution in connection with civil rights laws . . .

It is therefore perfectly clear where the Constitution stands. The Constitution stands for majority rule, but a majority rule which is carefully guarded—which requires the assent of both Houses, which is subject to a Presidential veto and subject to review by the courts.

We already have built-in protections for minorities and other groups, and long may we continue to have them.

Furthermore, by the so-called Connecticut compromise . . . we have equality of representation in the Senate of all States regardless of size. . . .

As a matter of fact, 17 States with only 8 percent of the population could, if acting in a bloc, under the existing rules of the Senate and under the rules as proposed by the Senator from Texas, by filibustering, tie up the Senate and prevent the representatives of the other 92 percent of the population from having their will.

What I am trying to say is that we already have built-in protections for minorities even under a majority provision; protection in the form of two Houses of Congress, protection in the form of the presidential veto; protection in the form of judicial review; and protection to the small States on the basis of equality of representation.

If on top of all this we have heaped upon us the power of a small group in the Senate to prevent us even from coming to a vote, there will be placed mighty and powerful chains upon us. . . .

We believe in full debate, full discussion—protracted debate, because many issues need to be made clear, not merely to the Senate, but to the country. But we believe that there is also the right of a majority at some time to reach a vote. The right of the majority to rule does not mean merely that when the ballot is cast the majority shall prevail. The right of the majority also to have a measure ultimately brought up for a vote is also an essential part of the right of majority rule. That is what we are contending for. . . .

Mr. TALMADGE. Mr. President——

The PRESIDING OFFICER. The Senator from Georgia.

Mr. TALMADGE. Mr. President, the proposal that the Senate adopt new rules involves considerably more than a mere question of the procedure to be followed in this Chamber.

Its ramifications extend to the very heart of our form of government and candor compels the conclusion that the effect of its approval would be to repudiate the Senate's assigned constitutional role.

It is vital, therefore, Mr. President, that this question be resolved not from the standpoint of any transient advantage which might accrue to some partisan group but rather on the basis of its implications for the future of constitutional, republican government in this Nation.

The United States Senate, in the light of history and the Constitution, is much more than another legislative body.

It is, in reality, a continuing council of States sitting as an integral part of the Federal establishment—a protective repository on the national level for the sovereignty of the sovereign States.

It was with plain design that our Founding Fathers created it as a watchman over all operations of our National Government.

And it was with deliberate intent that they conferred upon it the broadest powers to act as a checkmate on unwarranted centralization of authority.

Our far-seeing forefathers well realized that the House of Representatives would be both too large and too impermanent to fulfill those desired objectives.

They knew there could never be free debate in the House and that important bills would pass that chamber without sufficient study and deliberation.

And, perceiving those problems, they put their faith in the United States Senate and bestowed upon it the major responsibility for keeping faith with posterity.

To this date the Senate has kept that faith and I am humbly proud, Mr. President, to have the privilege of sitting in this honored body which has so faithfully discharged its appointed constitutional duty to serve as a bridge between the States and the Nation and a liaison between the past and the future.

The Senate has afforded continuity and stability to our Government.

The Senate has stood as a bulwark against usurpations of power.

Since it first effected its organization on April 6, 1789, there has not been a time in our national history when the Senate was not available as an organized body to answer the summons of the President and to fulfill its responsibilities in the transaction of public business.

Its first rules, adopted only 10 days after the Senate came into being, have continued in force without reaffirmation until amended or abolished by the Senate. . . .

And common sense dictates that they should not be subjected to whimsical tampering on the slightest provocation as it now is being insisted that we of this 86th Congress do.

At the outset, Mr. President, it is important that this Senate face the reality that the true purpose of those who would have it renounce its constitutional continuity is their desire to use that renunciation as a vehicle for destroying freedom of debate in this Chamber.

They are attacking not only the Senate itself but also the stature, perquisites and prerogatives of each Senator in national affairs and every other responsibility incident to the senatorship.

It is an attack which threatens the whole fabric of our form of government.

It is an attack which strikes at the very vitals of representative government.

It is an attack which aims a death blow to the States as political entities. . . .

Furthermore, Mr. President, I would warn this body that if the Senate elects to surrender on this issue, its action will mark the beginning of a sustained campaign to destroy the Senate as an institution of government. . . .

Should minority rights ever be trampled in the Senate there will remain only one remedy to those who do not happen at any given time to be a member of the majority; that is, affiliation with a multiplicity of splinter parties.

And I can think of no greater catastrophe befalling our Nation than the destruction of our two-party system.

It does not take much vision to see that under such circumstances any small militant minority exercising a balance of power could be thrust into a position where it could inflict great harm on the country. . . .

Mr. President, I consider this attack on the rules of the U.S. Senate far more serious than the fundamental constitutional objections to proposed force bills in the field of civil rights.

Under the guise of agitating for passage of such legislation, efforts are being made to alter our form of government.

It is not amiss to observe that throughout the course of history tyrants have seized power through the camouflage of some allegedly worthwhile cause. . . .

The sum and substance of all good legislation can be stated in one simple rule.

It is a rule about which all Americans should know.

It is the rule that under no circumstances should extreme and far-reaching Federal legislation affecting the basic rights of all the people of the Nation be adopted without substantial unanimity and support of all citizens.

National legislation should reflect mature, careful, and deliberate thought and discussion.

And, above all else, it should be conducive to unity, not division and disruption among our people.

Over the years the continuing goal of the Senate has been to promote such unity.

When we hear the cry of "majority rule" by proponents of majority cloture we should take into account a few simple facts about the origin and composition of the Senate.

It is impossible to apply to this body with any degree of accuracy the principle of popular majority rule as we usually consider it. The very composition of the U.S. Senate where all States have an equal vote prevents such an application.

It is possible for various combinations of 50 Senators to represent anywhere from 20 to 80 percent of the country's population.

All of the great injustices of history have been committed in the name of unchecked and unbridled majority rule.

The late Senator James A. Reed, of Missouri, in one of the most forceful speeches ever delivered before the Senate, observed with great truth that:

The majority crucified Jesus Christ.

The majority burned the Christians at the stake.

The majority drove the Jews into exile and to the ghetto.

The majority established slavery.

The majority chained to stakes and surrounded with circles of flame martyrs through all the ages of the world's history.

The majority jeered when Columbus said the world was round.

The majority threw him into a dungeon for having discovered a new world.

The majority said that Galileo must recant or that Galileo must go to prison.

The majority cut off the ears of John Pym because he dared advocate the liberty of the press . . .

It behooves us to examine carefully the Articles of Confederation, the Constitutional Convention and the Constitution itself . . .

The Articles of Confederation, standing alone, proved insufficient for successful operation of a central government. . . .

The States and their people were wary of the tyranny of central governments and despotic rulers. They were, by instinct, hesitant to surrender any portion of their newly won sovereign powers and their blood-won liberties.

The price at which they agreed to surrender a portion of them was the creation of the United States Senate. . . .

Though the Articles of Confederation afforded no basis for a worthwhile scheme of amendment or revision, many of the delegates nonetheless held fast to the principle that any new Constitution must include equality of State representation.

From first to last the Convention stood for the protection of private economic interests, a stronger central authority, a stabilized monetary system, orderly legal processes, and a republican form of government; but not for an unlimited democracy.

The motivating spirit of the Convention—not expressed, but clearly understood—was to make the Nation safe from unlimited democracy. Madison's own notes, as well as the papers of most of the other delegates, make such an intention unmistakable.

But, Mr. President, there remains one obvious defect in our Constitution.

There is nothing in the document to prevent the United States Senate from surrendering its powers and prerogatives by its own action.

Its only protection in that regard rests with the courage, conscience, and patriotism of its individual members and their collective determination to preserve the integrity of the senatorship.

Now, as . . . to . . . the Government of the United States, let us . . . dispose of one salient misconception.

Our country is a new experiment in government.

It is not a pure democracy.

It is not a pure republic.

Our national structure is a product of compromise.

It is a mixture of necessity.

It was welded by great men.

It is not like any other government on this earth.

It is strictly ours. . . .

Through the medium of free debate, Mr. President, the Senate provides the machinery by which all measures affecting the lives, fortunes, and sacred honor of the American people can be put to the critical test of unhurried examination by the collective intellect of a body expressly created as one of our governmental checks and balances.

Those who would destroy that right contend it imperils democracy and thwarts the wishes of the majority. In their zeal they forget that its very purpose is to provide a restraint upon the abuses of unbridled majority rule and, even more important, to protect the rights of the minorities of this Nation.

Our wise Founding Fathers were aware that the excesses of democracy can be as fearful in their consequences as are the excesses of totalitarianism. To safeguard against both extremes they gave us our republican form of government with its delicately contrived system of checks and balances of which freedom of debate in the Senate is at least an implied, if not actual, part. . . .

If the United States Senate commits suicide by repudiating the continuity of its rules or by moving another step closer to majority cloture, we will see the day when it is regarded by the American people as nothing more than a useless appendage of the House of Representatives. . . .

That is the reason, Mr. President, that I shall vote to uphold the integrity of the Senate as a continuing repository of State sovereignty and as an instrumentality through which individual freedoms are protected in the manner envisioned by the men who founded this great Nation.

The prayer of all Americans who cherish their freedom and their form of government will be, Mr. President, that the majority of the Senate will vote likewise. . . .

January 9, 1959

Mr. JOHNSON of Texas. Mr. President, I move to lay on the table the modified amendment of the Senator from New Mexico [Mr. ANDERSON], in the nature of a substitute for Senate Resolution 5.

I suggest the absence of a quorum.

The VICE PRESIDENT. The Secretary will call the roll.

The legislative clerk called the roll, and the following Senators answered to their names:

[*Ninety-seven of the ninety-eight senators were present.*]

Mr. MANSFIELD. I announce that the Senator from Oregon [Mr. NEUBERGER] is absent because of illness.

The VICE PRESIDENT. A quorum is present. . . .

The question is on agreeing to the motion of the Senator from Texas [Mr. JOHNSON] to lay on the table the modified amendment of the Senator from New Mexico, in the nature of a substitute for Senate Resolution 5. . . .

The motion is not debatable. The clerk will call the roll.

The Chief Clerk proceeded to call the roll.

Mr. CHURCH (when his name was called). On this vote I have a pair with the junior Senator from Oregon [Mr. NEUBERGER]. If he were present and voting he would vote "nay." If I were permitted to vote, I would vote "yea." I withhold my vote.

The rollcall was concluded.

The result was announced—yeas 60, nays 36, as follows:

[*The votes of the senators were listed.*]

So the motion of Mr. JOHNSON of Texas was agreed to.

Mr. JOHNSON of Texas. Mr. President, I move to reconsider the vote by which the motion to lay on the table was agreed to.

Mr. MANSFIELD. I move to lay that motion on the table.

The motion of the Senator from Montana to lay on the table was agreed to.

Mr. JOHNSON of Texas. Mr. President, I wish to inform the Senate that at about 12:10 o'clock we will proceed to the Chamber of the other body. After hearing the President's address, we plan to return to the Senate Chamber. Then it will be in order for Senators to introduce bills and submit resolutions.

We expect to ask the Senate to stay in session late this evening, in the hope that a vote can be reached on some of the amendments to rule XXII. If all Senators who wish to offer amendments to rule XXII will return to the Chamber, we shall consider whatever amendments may be called up and try to dispose of them as early as possible. . . .

Mr. JOHNSON of Texas. Mr. President, will the Chair state the pending business?

The PRESIDING OFFICER. The Chair lays before the Senate the unfinished business, Senate Resolution 5.

The Senate resumed the consideration of the resolution (S. Res. 5) proposing to amend Senate rules XXII and XXXII.

Mr. JOHNSON of Texas. Mr. President, I am prepared to vote on Senate Resolution 5. In the Senate we have discussed a proposed rule change every year for several years. It has been 10 years since rule XXII was revised.

I am informed some of my colleagues desire to deliberate in private before concluding just what course will be followed in connection with certain amendments. I am also informed many Senators would like to be free this evening to attend certain meetings they have arranged. But I am hopeful the Senate can proceed with dispatch on this very important matter and try to resolve it. . . . I am prepared to make a unanimous-consent request for next week, if that is satisfactory to the Senate. I should like to see if the minority would be willing to agree to have a session on Saturday, and a session on Monday, and proceed to vote on amendments after the morning hour on Monday, with 2 hours allotted to each amendment. I make such a unanimous consent request.

The PRESIDING OFFICER. Is there objection?

Mr. DOUGLAS. Mr. President, reserving the right to object, I wonder if the eminent and distinguished Senator from Texas would be willing to clarify his request a bit. Is he proposing that there be 2 hours on Monday on each amendment?

Mr. JOHNSON of Texas. Yes.

Mr. DOUGLAS. And how much time on final passage?

Mr. JOHNSON of Texas. Whatever is desirable—perhaps an hour to a side. Senators have heard these questions thoroughly discussed.

Mr. DOUGLAS. I wonder if the Senator from Texas would be willing to write out his proposal, so that we may see whether or not there is any fine print in it, and be able to study it in some detail.

Mr. JOHNSON of Texas. I shall be glad to do that, if

the Senator can see better than he can hear. [Laughter.]

Mr. DOUGLAS. I think it is always important to study the fine print in a document submitted by the Senator from Texas.

Mr. JOHNSON of Texas. The Senator reminds me of an old friend in the mountains of Texas. He was called Uncle Ezra. He went to see his doctor because he had great difficulty with his hearing. The doctor said it seemed that he was consuming too much alcohol—I do not associate the Senator from Illinois with alcohol—and that he would have to cut down on his drinking.

Uncle Ezra went home, and returned a month or two later. He said, "Doctor, my hearing is getting worse all the time."

The doctor said, "Uncle Ezra, did you cut down on your drinking?"

Uncle Ezra replied, "No; I have stepped it up a little."

The doctor said, "You are not following my instructions."

Uncle Ezra replied, "No."

"Why are you not following my instructions?" asked the doctor.

"Well," said Uncle Ezra, "I like what I drink so much better than what I hear." [Laughter.]

It may be that the Senator from Illinois likes what he sees much better than what he hears. However, I have been laboring under the assumption that Senators were seriously and genuinely interested in amending rule XXII. I realized that when Congress convened this year that would be the first order of business. I plead with Senators to roll up their sleeves and get on with the job. I am prepared to do so. . . .

Mr. DOUGLAS. Mr. President we are now moving into the crucial question which will decide whether we are to enact any civil rights legislation of an effective nature in this Congress, and perhaps even in this generation, or whether our efforts will be defeated by the proposed rule XXII which has been advanced by the Senator from Texas [Mr. JOHNSON].

[*Douglas then reviewed the history of the struggle over the filibuster from 1917 to 1949.*]

As I recall, . . . early in March, 1949 . . . the bipartisan alliance between the southern Senators and the conservative branch of the Republican Party . . . sprang into action, and there was circulated a round robin which pledged the signers to a tightening of the antifilibuster rule. As a result, rule XXII was amended, not in such a way as to make it easier to break a filibuster, but to make it a bit more difficult.

Mr. HOLLAND. Mr. President, at this point will the Senator from Illinois yield?

Mr. DOUGLAS. I yield for a question.

Mr. HOLLAND. Is it not true that the Senators who participated in that successful effort constituted a majority of the Senate?

Mr. DOUGLAS. Yes; that is true.

Mr. HOLLAND. I thought the Senator from Illinois had been calling for action by a majority of the Senate, when they wished it.

Mr. DOUGLAS. I was describing the sequence of events.

Mr. HOLLAND. But it is a fact, is it not, that a majority of the Senate elected to put an end to that fruitless debate, and did so by taking the action, as a majority of the Senate, which the distinguished Senator from Illinois has described? That is true, is it not?

Mr. DOUGLAS. Yes.

Mr. HOLLAND. Does the Senator from Illinois object to the right of a majority of the Senate to take action of that kind?

Mr. DOUGLAS. They had a right to take that action for the Senate which then was sitting. But in the argument which we advanced on yesterday, I believe we made it clear to all Members but the Senator from Florida, that that action was improper in so far as binding future Senates was concerned. . . .

Mr. HOLLAND. I understood that to be the Senator's position. I wish to address my next question to this point: Is it not true that in its action upon the Anderson amendment this morning, which was taken by a vote of 60 to 36 . . . the Senate took action by a decidedly strong majority?

Mr. DOUGLAS. Yes; that is true. However, I am

reluctant to believe that the vote this morning represents the opinion of the Senate or the country on the general question of filibuster. I believe it represents in the minds of many a parliamentary technicality. We tried to warn Senators that it was likely to be cited as a strong vote in favor of protecting the filibuster. However I am afraid there were some Senators, particularly new Members, who did not fully realize the significance of the vote they cast. . . .

If we proceed under rule XXII, as proposed by the Senator from Texas [Mr. JOHNSON], the two-thirds requirement is sufficiently effective to protect a filibuster on matters to which a given section of the country, although a minority of the whole Nation, is opposed. . . .

I think it should be crystal clear by now that the attempt to say what was said today—that a majority can at any time pass a measure if it is put to a vote—begs the question.

The point is that with rules governing a filibuster it is impossible to bring many vital measures to a vote. There will be interminable discussion. It will not be possible to get cloture, and the measure will die, even though a majority—and a large majority—of the Nation desires it.

Thus I say, so far as rule XXII is concerned, that two-thirds is about as effective as unanimous consent. . . .

January 12, 1959

AMENDMENT OF THE RULES

The Senate resumed the consideration of the resolution (S. Res. 5) proposing to amend Senate rules XXII and XXXII. . . .

The PRESIDING OFFICER. The resolution is open to amendment.

Mr. JAVITS and Mr. CASE of South Dakota addressed the Chair.

The PRESIDING OFFICER. The Senator from New York is recognized.

Mr. JAVITS. Mr. President, I call up my amendment and ask that it be stated.

The PRESIDING OFFICER. The amendment will be stated for the information of the Senate.

The LEGISLATIVE CLERK. On page 2, lines 2 and 3, it is proposed to strike out the words "as provided in these rules."

The PRESIDING OFFICER. The Senate will be in order so that the Senator from New York may be recognized and proceed so as to be heard. The Chair recognizes the Senator from New York. How much time does the Senator yield himself?

Mr. JAVITS. Ten minutes, Mr. President.

The PRESIDING OFFICER. The Senator from New York is recognized for 10 minutes. . . .

Mr. JAVITS. The Johnson resolution—and this is one point which has not been adequately discussed—purports only to continue the rules of the Senate from Congress to Congress. It so states in so many words. But it also purports to prevent us from changing the rules unless we comply with these rules. Let us read specifically the provision of section 2 of the Johnson resolution, with the change I propose to make. Section 2 reads:

The rules of the Senate shall continue from one Congress to the next Congress unless they are changed, as provided in these rules.

By my amendment I seek to excise the words "as provided in these rules." Hence the section, if my amendment should prevail, would read as follows:

The rules of the Senate shall continue from one Congress to the next Congress unless they are changed.

The physical situation would then be that we would attend the opening session of a new Congress, as we did the other day; and the rules of the Senate would be in effect, if my amendment were adopted, except that if an effort were made to amend the rules, that effort would be under constitutional safeguards of normal parliamentary procedure, rather than under these rules. . . .

Mr. CASE of South Dakota. Mr. President, will the Senator yield?

Mr. JAVITS. I yield.

Mr. CASE of South Dakota. . . . Why did the able Senator from New York propose to put the period after the word "change"? Why did he not put it after "next Congress"? It seems to me that the language which would be left would be susceptible of two interpretations. It could be said that obviously the rules continue unless they are changed. Suppose the period were to be placed after the word "Congress," so that the sentence would read:

The rules of the Senate shall continue from one Congress to the next Congress.

Mr. JAVITS. I amend my amendment to that effect, so that it will now read to strike out, on page 2, line 2, the words "unless they are changed as provided in these rules." The period will appear after the word "Congress" in line 2. I accept that suggestion. I think it is better English. . . .

[*After extensive further discussion, the debate closed in the following manner:*]

Mr. DIRKSEN. Mr. President, I yield back the remainder of my time.

Mr. JOHNSON of Texas. I suggest the absence of a quorum.

The PRESIDING OFFICER. All time having expired or been yielded back, the Secretary will call the roll.

The question is on agreeing to the resolution of the Senator from Texas [Mr. JOHNSON]. The yeas and nays have been ordered, and the clerk will call the roll.

The legislative clerk proceeded to call the roll.

Mr. YOUNG of North Dakota (when his name was called). On this vote I have a pair with the senior Senator from New Hampshire [Mr. BRIDGES]. If he were present and voting, he would vote "yea"; if I were permitted to vote, I would vote "nay." I therefore withhold my vote.

The rollcall was concluded.

Mr. MANSFIELD. I announce that the Senator from Oregon [Mr. NEUBERGER] is absent because of illness.

I further announce that, if present and voting the Senator from Oregon [Mr. NEUBERGER], would vote "yea."

Mr. DIRKSEN. I announce that the Senator from New Hampshire [Mr. BRIDGES] is absent on official business and his pair has been previously announced by the Senator from North Dakota [Mr. YOUNG].

The Senator from South Dakota [Mr. MUNDT] is absent on official business and if present and voting, he would vote "yea."

The result was announced—yeas 72, nays 22, as follows:

YEAS—72

Aiken
Allott
Anderson
Bartlett
Beall
Bennett
Bible
Bush
Butler
Byrd, W. Va.
Cannon
Capehart
Carlson
Carroll
Case, N.J.
Case, S. Dak.
Chavez
Church
Clark
Cooper
Cotton
Curtis
Dirksen
Dodd
Dworshak
Engle
Ervin
Frear
Goldwater
Gore
Green
Gruening
Hartke
Hayden
Hennings
Hickenlooper
Holland
Hruska
Humphrey
Jackson
Johnson, Tex.
Jordan
Keating
Kefauver
Kennedy
Kerr
Magnuson
Mansfield
Martin
McCarthy
McGee
Monroney
Morton
Moss
Murray
Muskie
O'Mahoney
Pastore
Prouty
Proxmire
Randolph
Saltonstall
Schoeppel
Scott
Smathers
Smith
Symington
Wiley
Williams, N.J.
Williams, Del.
Yarborough
Young, Ohio

NAYS—22

Byrd, Va.
Douglas
Eastland
Ellender
Fulbright
Hart
Hill
Javits
Johnston, S.C.
Kuchel
Langer
Lausche
Long
McClellan
McNamara
Morse
Robertson
Russell
Sparkman
Stennis
Talmadge
Thurmond

NOT VOTING—4

Bridges
Mundt
Neuberger
Young, N. Dak.

So the resolution (S. Res. 5) was agreed to.

Mr. DIRKSEN. Mr. President, I move to reconsider the vote by which the resolution was agreed to.

Mr. JOHNSON of Texas. I move to lay that motion on the table.

The motion to lay on the table was agreed to.

McGrain v. Daugherty*

As a result of the Teapot Dome scandals in the Harding Administration, the Senate undertook an investigation of the Justice Department. The investigating committee issued a warrant for the arrest of Mally S. Daugherty, brother of the Attorney General, who had failed to respond to its subpoena. Daugherty challenged this action on the grounds that Congress had no power under the Constitution to conduct investigations and compel testimony.

In view of the wide and significant use of Congressional investigations, especially in recent years, and the reliance placed on them by Congress in its exercise of its powers of legislation and control of the executive, the importance of the Court's decision in this case is readily apparent.

Another case bearing directly on the authority and the composition of Congress is Colegrove v. Green *which is reprinted on pp. 194-197 below.*

Mr. Justice Van Devanter delivered the opinion of the court, saying, in part:

This is an appeal from the final order in a proceeding in *habeas corpus* discharging a recusant witness held in custody under process of attachment issued from the United States Senate in the course of an investigation which it was making of the administration of the Department of Justice. . . .

The principal questions involved are of unusual importance and delicacy. They are (a) whether the Senate—or the House of Representatives, both being on the same plane in this regard—has power, through its own process, to compel a private individual to appear before it or one of its committees and give testimony needed to enable it efficiently to exercise a legislative function

* 273 U.S. 135 (1927).

belonging to it under the Constitution, and (b) whether it sufficiently appears that the process was being employed in this instance to obtain testimony for that purpose . . .

The Constitution provides for a Congress consisting of a Senate and House of Representatives and invests it with "all legislative powers" granted to the United States, and with power "to make all laws which shall be necessary and proper" for carrying into execution these powers and "all other powers" vested by the Constitution in the United States or in any department or officer thereof. . . . But there is no provision expressly investing either house with power to make investigations and exact testimony to the end that it may exercise its legislative function advisedly and effectively. So the question arises whether this power is so far incidental to the legislative function as to be implied.

In actual legislative practice power to secure needed information by such means has long been treated as an attribute of the power to legislate. It was so regarded in the British Parliament and in the Colonial legislatures before the American Revolution; and a like view has prevailed and been carried into effect in both houses of Congress and in most of the state legislatures.

This power was both asserted and exerted by the House of Representatives in 1792, when it appointed a select committee to inquire into the St. Clair expedition and authorized the committee to send for necessary persons, papers and records. Mr. Madison, who had taken an important part in framing the Constitution only five years before, and four of his associates in that work, were members of the House of Representatives at the time, and all voted for the inquiry . . . Other exertions of the power by the House of Representatives, as also by the Senate, are shown in the citations already made. Among those by the Senate, the inquiry ordered in 1859 respecting the raid by John Brown and his adherents on the armory and arsenal of the United States at Harper's Ferry is of special significance. The resolution directing the inquiry authorized the committee to send for persons and papers, to inquire into the facts pertaining to the raid and the means by which it was organized and supported, and to report what legislation, if any, was necessary to preserve the peace of the country and protect the public property. The resolution was briefly discussed and adopted without opposition . . . Later on the committee reported that Thaddeus Hyatt, although subpoenaed to appear as a witness, had refused to do so; where-upon the Senate ordered that he be attached and brought before it to answer for his refusal. When he was brought in he answered by challenging the power of the Senate to direct the inquiry and exact testimony to aid it in exercising its legislative function. The question of power thus presented was thoroughly discussed by several senators—Mr. Sumner of Massachusetts taking the lead in denying the power and Mr. Fessenden of Maine in supporting it. Sectional and party lines were put aside and the question was debated and determined with special regard to principle and precedent. The vote was taken on a resolution pronouncing the witness's answer insufficient and directing that he be committed until he should signify that he was ready and willing to testify. The resolution was adopted—44 senators voting for it and 10 against . . .

The deliberate solution of the question on that occasion has been accepted and followed on other occasions by both houses of Congress, and never has been rejected or questioned by either.

The state courts quite generally have held that the power to legislate carries with it by necessary implication ample authority to obtain information needed in the rightful exercise of that power, and to employ compulsory process for the purpose. [The court cites examples.] . . .

We have referred to the practice of the two houses of Congress; and we now shall notice some significant congressional enactments. May 3, 1798, . . . Congress provided that oaths or affirmations might be administered to witnesses by the President of the Senate, the Speaker of the House of Representatives, the chairman of a committee of the whole, or the chairman of a select committee, "in any case under their examination." February 8, 1817, . . . it enlarged that provision so as to include the chairman of a standing committee. January 24, 1857, . . . it passed "An Act more effectually to enforce the attendance of witnesses on the summons of either house of Congress, and to compel them to discover testimony." This act provided, first, that any person summoned as a witness to give testimony or produce papers in any matter under inquiry before either house of Congress, or any committee of either house, who should wilfully make default, or, if appearing, should refuse to answer any question pertinent to the inquiry, should . . . be deemed guilty of a misdemeanor . . . ; and secondly, that no person should be excused from giving evidence in such an inquiry on the ground that it might tend to incriminate or disgrace him, nor be held to answer criminally, or be subjected to any penalty or forfeiture, for any fact or act as to which he was required to testify, excepting that he might be subjected to prosecution for perjury committed while so testifying . . . These enactments . . . show very plainly that Congress intended thereby (a) to recognize the power of either house to institute inquiries and exact evidence touching subjects within its jurisdiction and on which it was disposed to act; (b) to recognize that such inquiries may be conducted through committees; (c) to subject defaulting and contumacious witnesses to indictment and punishment in the courts, and thereby to enable either house to exert the power of inquiry "more effectually"; and (d) to open the way for obtaining evidence in such an inquiry, which otherwise could not be obtained, by exempting witnesses required to give evidence therein from criminal and penal prosecutions in respect of matters disclosed by their evidence.

Four decisions of this Court are cited and more or less relied on, and we now turn to them.

The first decision was in *Anderson* v. *Dunn,* 6 Wheat. 204. The question there was whether, under the Constitution, the House of Representatives has power to attach and punish a person other than a member for contempt of its authority—in fact, an attempt to bribe one of its members. The Court regarded the power as essential to the effective exertion of other powers expressly granted, and therefore as implied. . . .

The next decision was in *Kilbourn* v. *Thompson,* 103 U.S. 168. The question there was whether the House of

Representatives had exceeded its power in directing one of its committees to make a particular investigation. The decision was that it had. The principles announced and applied in the case are—that neither house or Congress possesses a "general power of making inquiry into the private affairs of the citizen"; that the power actually possessed is limited to inquiries relating to matters of which the particular house "has jurisdiction" and in respect of which it rightfully may take other action; that if the inquiry relates to "a matter wherein relief or redress could be had only by a judicial proceeding" it is not within the range of this power, but must be left to the courts, conformably to the constitutional separation of governmental powers; and that for the purpose of determining the essential character of the inquiry recourse may be had to the resolution or order under which it is made. The court examined the resolution which was the basis of the particular inquiry, and ascertained there-from that the inquiry related to a private real-estate pool or partnership in the District of Columbia. Jay Cook & Co. had had an interest in the pool, but had become bankrupts, and their estate was in course of administration in a federal bankruptcy court in Pennsylvania. The United States was one of their creditors. The trustee in the bankruptcy proceeding had effected a settlement of the bankrupts' interest in the pool, and of course his action was subject to examination and approval or disapproval by the bankruptcy court. Some of the creditors, including the United States, were dissatisfied with the settlement. In these circumstances, disclosed in the preamble, the resolution directed the committee "to inquire into the matter and history of said real-estate pool and the character of said settlement, with the amount of property involved in which Jay Cook & Co. were interested, and the amount paid or to be paid in said settlement, with power to send for persons and papers and report to the House." The Court pointed out that the resolution contained no suggestion of contemplated legislation; that the matter was one in respect to which no valid legislation could be had; that the bankrupts' estate and the trustee's settlement were still pending in the bankruptcy court; and that the United States and other creditors were free to press their claims in that proceeding. And on these grounds the Court held that in undertaking the investigation "the House of Representatives not only exceeded the limit of its own authority, but assumed power which could only be properly exercised by another branch of the government, because it was in its nature clearly judicial." . . .

Next in order is *In re Chapman,* 166 U.S. 661. The inquiry there in question was conducted under a resolution of the Senate and related to charges, published in the press, that senators were yielding to corrupt influences in considering a tariff bill then before the Senate and were speculating in stocks the value of which would be affected by pending amendments to the bill. Chapman appeared before the committee in response to a subpoena, but refused to answer questions pertinent to the inquiry, and was indicted and convicted under the act of 1857 for his refusal. The Court sustained the constitutional validity of the act of 1857, and, after referring to the constitutional provision empowering either house to punish its members for disorderly behavior and by a vote of two-thirds to expel a member, held that the inquiry related to the integrity and fidelity of senators in the discharge of their duties, and therefore to a matter "within the range of the constitutional powers of the Senate" and in respect of which it could compel witnesses to appear and testify. In overruling an objection that the inquiry was without any defined or admissible purpose, in that the preamble and resolution made no reference to any contemplated expulsion, censure, or other action by the Senate, the Court held that they adequately disclosed a subject-matter of which the Senate had jurisdiction, that it was not essential that the Senate declare in advance what it meditated doing, and that the assumption could not be indulged that the Senate was making the inquiry without a legitimate object.

The case is relied on here as fully sustaining the power of either house to conduct investigations and exact testimony from witnesses for legislative purposes. In the course of the opinion (p. 671) it is said that disclosures by witnesses may be compelled constitutionally "to enable the respective bodies to discharge their legitimate functions, and that it was to effect this that the act of 1857 was passed"; and also "We grant that Congress could not divest itself, or either of its houses, of the essential and inherent power to punish for contempt, in cases to which the power of either house properly extended; but, because Congress, by the act of 1857, sought to aid each of the houses in the discharge of its constitutional functions, it does not follow that any delegation of the power in each to punish for contempt was involved." The terms "legitimate functions" and "constitutional functions" are broad and might well be regarded as including the legislative function, but as the case in hand did not call for any expression respecting that function, it hardly can be said that these terms were purposely used as including it.

The latest case is *Marshall* v. *Gordon*, 243 U.S. 521. The question there was whether the House of Representatives exceeded its power in punishing, as for a contempt of its authority, a person—not a member—who had written, published and sent to the chairman of one of its committees an ill-tempered and irritating letter respecting the action and purposes of the committee . . . The Court recognized distinctly that the House of Representatives has implied power to punish a person not a member for contempt, . . . but held that its action in this instance was without constitutional justification. The decision was put on the ground that the letter, while offensive and vexatious, was not calculated or likely to affect the House in any of its proceedings or in the exercise of any of its functions—in short, that the act which was punished as a contempt was not of such a character as to bring it within the rule that an express power draws after it others which are necessary and appropriate to give effect to it.

While these cases are not decisive of the question we are considering, they definitely settle two propositions which we recognize as entirely sound and having a bearing on its solution: One, that the two houses of Congress, in their separate relations, possess not only such powers as are expressly granted to them by the Constitution, but such auxiliary powers as are necessary and appropriate to make the express powers effective; and, the other, that neither house is invested with "general" power to inquire into private affairs and compel disclosures, but only with such limited power of inquiry as is shown to exist when the rule of constitutional interpretation just stated is rightly applied. . . .

With this review of the legislative practice, congressional enactments and court decisions, we proceed to a statement of our conclusions on the question.

We are of opinion that the power of inquiry—with process to enforce it—is an essential and appropriate auxiliary to the legislative function. It was so regarded and employed in American legislatures before the Constitution was framed and ratified. Both houses of Congress took this view of it early in their history—the House of Representatives with the approving votes of Mr. Madison and other members whose service in the convention which framed the Constitution gives special significance to their action—and both houses have employed the power accordingly up to the present time. The acts of 1798 and 1857, judged by their comprehensive terms, were intended to recognize the existence of this power in both houses and to enable them to employ it "more effectually" than before. So, when their practice in the matter is appraised according to the circumstance in which it was begun and to those in which it has been continued, it falls nothing short of a practical construction, long continued, of the constitutional provisions respecting their powers, and therefore should be taken as fixing the meaning of those provisions, if otherwise doubtful.

We are further of opinion that the provisions are not of doubtful meaning, but, . . . are intended to be effectively exercised, and therefore to carry with them such auxiliary powers as are necessary and appropriate to that end. While the power to exact information in aid of the legislative function was not involved in those cases, the rule of interpretation applied there is applicable here. A legislative body cannot legislate wisely or effectively in the absence of information respecting the conditions which the legislation is intended to affect or change; and where the legislative body does not itself possess the requisite information—which not infrequently is true—recourse must be had to others who do possess it. Experience has taught that mere requests for such information often are unavailing, and also that information which is volunteered is not always accurate or complete; so some means of compulsion are essential to obtain what is needed. All this was true before and when the Constitution was framed and adopted. In that period the power of inquiry—with enforcing process—was regarded and employed as a necessary and appropriate attribute of the power to legislate—indeed, was treated as inhering in it. Thus there is ample warrant for thinking, as we do, that the constitutional provisions which commit the legislative function to the two houses are intended to include this attribute to the end that the function may be effectively exercised.

The contention is earnestly made on behalf of the witness that this power of inquiry, if sustained, may be abusively and oppressively exerted. If this be so, it affords no ground for denying the power. The same contention might be directed against the power to legislate, and of course would be unavailing. . . . But . . . a witness rightfully may refuse to answer where the bounds of the power are exceeded or the questions are not pertinent to the matter under inquiry.

We come now to the questions whether it sufficiently appears that the purpose for which the witness's testimony was sought was to obtain information in aid of the legislative function. The court below answered the question in the negative. . . .

We are of opinion that the court's ruling on this question was wrong, and that it sufficiently appears, . . . that the object of the investigation and of the effort to secure the witness's testimony was to obtain information for legislative purposes.

It is quite true that the resolution directing the investigation does not in terms avow that it is intended to be in aid of legislation; but it does show that the subject to be investigated was the administration of the Department of Justice—whether its functions were being properly discharged or were being neglected or misdirected, and particularly whether the Attorney General and his assistants were performing or neglecting their duties in respect of the institution and prosecution of proceedings to punish crimes and enforce appropriate remedies against the wrongdoers—specific instances of alleged neglect being recited. Plainly the subject was one on which legislation could be had and would be materially aided by the information which the investigation was calculated to elicit. This becomes manifest when it is reflected that the functions of the Department of Justice, the powers and duties of the Attorney General and the duties of his assistants, are all subject to regulation by congressional legislation, and that the department is maintained and its activities are carried on under such appropriations as in the judgment of Congress are needed from year to year.

The only legitimate object the Senate could have in ordering the investigation was to aid it in legislating; and we think the subject-matter was such that the presumption should be indulged that this was the real object. An express avowal of the object would have been better; but in view of the particular subject-matter was not indispensable . . .

While we rest our conclusion respecting the object of the investigation on the grounds just stated; it is well to observe that this view of what was intended is not new, but was shown in the [Senate] debate on the resolution . . .

We conclude that the investigation was ordered for a legitimate object; that the witness wrongfully refused to appear and testify before the committee and was lawfully attached; that the Senate is entitled to have him give testimony pertinent to the inquiry, either at its bar or before the committee; and that the district court erred in discharging him from custody under the attachment . . .

Final order reversed.

Mr. Justice Stone did not participate in the consideration or decision of the case . . .

— 4 —

THE PRESIDENCY

THE PRESIDENT HAS NO UNDEFINED RESIDUUM OF POWER *

By William Howard Taft

The use made of the powers of the Presidency by its incumbents has varied considerably. A number of Presidents have expressed views on the proper role of that office in the American governmental system. The following three selections present a representative choice of such views.

The true view of the Executive functions is, as I conceive it, that the President can exercise no power which cannot be fairly and reasonably traced to some specific grant of power or justly implied and included within such express grant as proper and necessary to its exercise. Such specific grant must be either in the Federal Constitution or in an act of Congress passed in pursuance thereof. There is no undefined residuum of power which he can exercise because it seems to him to be in the public interest . . . The grants of Executive power are necessarily in general terms in order not to embarrass the Executive within the field of action plainly marked for him, but his jurisdiction must be justified and vindicated by affirmative constitutional or statutory provision, or it does not exist. There have not been wanting, however, eminent men in high public office holding a different view

* From *Our Chief Magistrate and His Powers,* Columbia University Press, New York, 1916, pp. 139-157. Reprinted by permission.

and who have insisted upon the necessity for an undefined residuum of Executive power in the public interest . . .

Mr. Garfield, when Secretary of the Interior, under Mr. Roosevelt, in his final report to Congress in reference to the power of the Executive over the public domain, said:

> Full power under the Constitution was vested in the Executive Branch of the Government and the extent to which that power may be exercised is governed wholly by the discretion of the Executive unless any specific act has been prohibited either by the Constitution or by legislation. . . .

My judgment is that the view of Mr. Garfield and Mr. Roosevelt,* ascribing an undefined residuum of power to the President is an unsafe doctrine and that it might lead under emergencies to results of an arbitrary character, doing irremediable injustice to private right. The mainspring of such a view is that the Executive is charged with responsibility for the welfare of all the people in a general way, that he is to play the part of a Universal Providence and set all things right, and that anything that in his judgment will help the people he ought to do, unless he is expressly forbidden not to do it. The wide field of action that this would give to the Executive one can hardly limit. . . .

The Executive power, . . . is limited, so far as it is possible to limit such a power consistent with that discretion and promptness of action that are essential to preserve the interests of the public in times of emergency, or legislative neglect or inaction.

There is little danger of the public weal from the tyranny or reckless character of a President who is not sustained by the people. The absence of popular support will certainly in the course of two years withdraw from him the sympathetic action of at least one House of Congress, and by the control that that House has over appropriations, the Executive arm can be paralyzed, unless he resorts to a coup d'état, which means impeachment, conviction and deposition. The only danger in the action of the Executive under the present limitations and

* See pp. 160-163 below for Roosevelt's views.—Ed. note.

lack of limitation of his powers is when his popularity is such that he can be sure of the support of the electorate and therefore of Congress, and when the majority in the legislative halls respond with alacrity and sycophancy to his will. This condition cannot probably be long continued. We have had Presidents who felt the public pulse with accuracy, who played their parts upon the political stage with histrionic genius and commanded the people almost as if they were an army and the President their Commander-in-Chief. Yet in all these cases, the good sense of the people has ultimately prevailed and no danger has been done to our political structure and the reign of law has continued. In such times when the Executive power seems to be all prevailing, there have always been men in this free and intelligent people of ours, who apparently courting political humiliation and disaster have registered protest against this undue Executive domination and this use of the Executive power and popular support to perpetuate itself.

The cry of Executive domination is often entirely unjustified, as when the President's commanding influence only grows out of a proper cohesion of a party and its recognition of the necessity for political leadership; but the fact that Executive domination is regarded as a useful ground for attack upon a successful administration, even when there is no ground for it, is itself proof of the dependence we may properly place upon the sanity and clear perceptions of the people in avoiding its baneful effects when there is real danger. Even if a vicious precedent is set by the Executive, and injustice done, it does not have the same bad effect that an improper precedent of a court may have, for one President does not consider himself bound by the policies or constitutional views of his predecessors.

The Constitution does give the President wide discretion and great power, and it ought to do so. It calls from him activity and energy to see that within his proper sphere he does what his great responsibilities and opportunities require. He is no figurehead, and it is entirely proper that an energetic and active clear-sighted people, who, when they have work to do, wish it done well, should be willing to rely upon their judgment in selecting their Chief

Agent, and having selected him, should entrust to him all the power needed to carry out their governmental purpose, great as it may be . . .

THE PRESIDENT IS STEWARD OF THE PEOPLE *

By Theodore Roosevelt

The most important factor in getting the right spirit in my Administration, next to the insistence upon courage, honesty, and a genuine democracy of desire to serve the plain people, was my insistence upon the theory that the executive power was limited only by specific restrictions and prohibitions appearing in the Constitution or imposed by the Congress under its Constitutional powers. My view was that every executive officer, and above all every executive officer in high position, was a steward of the people bound actively and affirmatively to do all he could for the people, and not to content himself with the negative merit of keeping his talents undamaged in a napkin. I declined to adopt the view that what was imperatively necessary for the Nation could not be done by the President unless he could find some specific authorization to do it. My belief was that it was not only his right but his duty to do anything that the needs of the Nation demanded unless such action was forbidden by the Constitution or by the laws. Under this interpretation of executive power I did and caused to be done many things not previously done by the President and the heads of the departments. I did not usurp power, but I did greatly broaden the use of executive power. In other words, I acted for the public welfare, I acted for the common well-being of all our people, whenever and in whatever manner was necessary, unless prevented by direct constitutional or legislative prohibition. I did not care a rap for the mere form and show of power; I cared immensely for the use that could be made of the substance . . .

* From *Theodore Roosevelt—An Autobiography,* Macmillan, New York, 1919, pp. 388-389, 394-399. Reprinted by permission of Charles Scribner's Sons, the present copyright holder.

It was again and again necessary to assert the position of the President as steward of the whole people. . . .

There have long been two schools of political thought, upheld with equal sincerity. The division has not normally been along political, but temperamental, lines. The course I followed, of regarding the executive as subject only to the people, and, under the Constitution, bound to serve the people affirmatively in cases where the Constitution does not explicitly forbid him to render the service, was substantially the course followed by both Andrew Jackson and Abraham Lincoln. Other honorable and well-meaning Presidents, such as James Buchanan, took the opposite and, as it seems to me, narrowly legalistic view that the President is the servant of Congress rather than of the people, and can do nothing, no matter how necessary it be to act, unless the Constitution explicitly commands the action. Most able lawyers who are past middle age take this view, and so do large numbers of well meaning, respectable citizens. My successor in office took this, the Buchanan, view of the President's powers and duties. . . .

I acted on the theory that the President could at any time in his discretion withdraw from entry any of the public lands of the United States and reserve the same for forestry, for water-power sites, for irrigation, and other public purposes. Without such action it would have been impossible to stop the activity of the land thieves. No one ventured to test its legality by lawsuit. My successor, however, himself questioned it, and referred the matter to Congress. Again Congress showed its wisdom by passing a law which gave the President the power which he had long exercised, and of which my successor had shorn himself.

Perhaps the sharp difference between what may be called the Lincoln-Jackson and the Buchanan-Taft schools, in their views of the power and duties of the President, may be best illustrated by comparing the attitude of my successor toward his Secretary of the Interior, Mr. Ballinger, when the latter was accused of gross misconduct in office, with my attitude towards my chiefs of department and other subordinate officers. More than once while I was President my officials were attacked by

Congress, generally because these officials did their duty well and fearlessly. In every such case I stood by the official and refused to recognize the right of Congress to interfere with me excepting by impeachment or in other Constitutional manner. On the other hand, wherever I found the officer unfit for his position I promptly removed him, even though the most influential men in Congress fought for his retention. The Jackson-Lincoln view is that a President who is fit to do good work should be able to form his own judgment as to his own subordinates, and, above all, of subordinates standing highest and in closest and most intimate touch with him. My secretaries and their subordinates were responsible to me, and I accepted the responsibility for all their deeds. As long as they were satisfactory to me I stood by them against every critic or assailant, within or without Congress; and as for getting Congress to make up my mind for me about them, the thought would have been inconceivable to me. My successor took the opposite, or Buchanan, view when he permitted and requested Congress to pass judgment on the charges made against Mr. Ballinger as an executive officer. These charges were made to the President; the President had the facts before him and could get at them at any time, and he alone had power to act if the charges were true. However, he permitted and requested Congress to investigate Mr. Ballinger. The party minority of the committee that investigated him, and one member of the majority, declared that the charges were well founded and that Mr. Ballinger should be removed. The other members of the majority declared the charges ill founded. The President abode by the view of the majority. Of course believers in the Jackson-Lincoln theory of the Presidency would not be content with this town meeting majority and minority method of determining by another branch of the Government what it seems the especial duty of the President himself to determine for himself in dealing with his own subordinate in his own department.

There are many worthy people who reprobate the Buchanan method as a matter of history, but who in actual life reprobate still more strongly the Jackson-Lincoln method when it is put into practice. These persons conscientiously believe that the President should solve every doubt in favor of inaction as against action, that he should construe strictly and narrowly the Constitutional grant of powers both to the National Government, and to the President within the National Government. In addition, however, to the men who conscientiously believe in this course from high, although as I hold misguided, motives, there are many men who affect to believe in it merely because it enables them to attack and to try to hamper, for partisan or personal reasons, an executive whom they dislike. There are other men in whom, especially when they are themselves in office, practical adherence to the Buchanan principle represents not well-thought-out devotion to an unwise course, but simple weakness of character and desire to avoid trouble and responsibility. Unfortunately, in practice it makes little difference which class of ideas actuates the President, who by his action sets a cramping precedent. Whether he is highminded and wrongheaded or merely infirm of purpose, whether he means well feebly or is bound by a mischievous misconception of the powers and duties of the National Government and of the President, the effect of his actions is the same. The President's duty is to act so that he himself and his subordinates shall be able to do efficient work for the people, and this efficient work he and they cannot do if Congress is permitted to undertake the task of making up his mind for him as to how he shall perform what is clearly his sole duty.

THE PRESIDENT IS ALONE AT THE TOP *

By John F. Kennedy

The history of this nation—its brightest and its bleakest pages—has been written largely in terms of the different views our Presidents have had of the Presidency itself . . .

In the decade that lies ahead—in the challenging, revolutionary Sixties—the American Presidency will demand more than ringing manifestoes issued from the

* From a speech delivered January 14, 1960, at the National Press Club, Washington, D.C.

rear of the battle. It will demand that the President place himself in the very thick of the fight, that he care passionately about the fate of the people he leads, that he be willing to serve them at the risk of incurring their momentary displeasure.

Whatever the political affiliation of our next President, whatever his views may be on all the issues and problems that rush in upon us, he must above all be the Chief Executive in every sense of the word. He must be prepared to exercise the fullest powers of his office—all that are specified and some that are not. He must master complex problems as well as receive one-page memoranda. He must originate action as well as study groups. He must reopen the channels of communication between the world of thought and the seat of power.

Ulysses Grant considered the President "a purely administrative officer." If he administered the Government departments efficiently, delegated his functions smoothly, and performed his ceremonies of state with decorum and grace, no more was to be expected of him. But that is not the place the Presidency was meant to have in American life. The President is alone, at the top—the loneliest job there is, as Harry Truman has said.

If there is destructive dissension among the services, he alone can step in and straighten it out—instead of waiting for unanimity. If administrative agencies are not carrying out their mandate—if a brushfire threatens some part of the globe—he alone can act, without waiting for the Congress. If his farm program fails, he alone deserves the blame, not his Secretary of Agriculture.

"The President is at liberty, both in law and conscience, to be as big a man as he can." So wrote Professor Woodrow Wilson. But President Woodrow Wilson discovered that to be a big man in the White House inevitably brings cries of dictatorship.

So did Lincoln and Jackson and the two Roosevelts. And so may the next occupant of that office, if he is the man the times demand. But how much better it would be, in the turbulent Sixties, to have a Roosevelt or a Wilson than to have another James Buchanan, cringing in the White House, afraid to move.

Nor can we afford a Chief Executive who is praised

primarily for what he did not do, the disasters he prevented, the bills he vetoed—a President wishing his subordinates would produce more missiles or build more schools. We will need instead what the Constitution envisioned: a Chief Executive who is the vital center of action in our whole scheme of Government.

This includes the legislative process as well. The President cannot afford—for the sake of the office as well as the nation—to be another Warren G. Harding, described by one backer as a man who "would, when elected, sign whatever bill the Senate sent him—and not send bills for the Senate to pass." Rather he must know when to lead the Congress, when to consult it and when he should act alone.

Having served fourteen years in the Legislative Branch, I would not look with favor upon its domination by the Executive. Under our Government of "power as the rival of power," to use Hamilton's phrase, Congress must not surrender its responsibilities. But neither should it dominate. However large its share in the formulation of domestic programs, it is the President alone who must make the major decisions of our foreign policy.

That is what the Constitution wisely commands. And even domestically, the President must initiate policies and devise laws to meet the needs of the nation. And he must be prepared to use all the resources of his office to insure the enactment of that legislation—even when conflict is the result.

By the end of his term Theodore Roosevelt was not popular in the Congress—particularly when he criticized an amendment to the Treasury appropriation which forbade the use of Secret Service men to investigate Congressmen!

And the feeling was mutual Roosevelt saying: "I do not much admire the Senate, because it is such a helpless body when efficient work is to be done."

And Woodrow Wilson was even more bitter after his frustrating quarrels—asked if he might run for the Senate in 1920, he replied: "Outside of the United States, the Senate does not amount to a damn. And inside the United States, the Senate is mostly despised. They haven't had a thought down there in fifty years."

But, however bitter their farewells, the facts of the matter are that Roosevelt and Wilson did get things done—not only through their Executive powers but through the Congress as well. Calvin Coolidge, on the other hand, departed from Washington with cheers of Congress still ringing in his ears. But when his World Court bill was under fire on Capitol Hill he sent no messages, gave no encouragement to the bill's leaders and paid little or no attention to the whole proceeding—and the cause of world justice was set back.

To be sure, Coolidge had held the usual White House breakfasts with Congressional leaders—but they were aimed, as he himself said, at "good fellowship," not a discussion of "public business." And at his press conferences, according to press historians, where he preferred to talk about the local flower show and its exhibits, reporters who finally extracted from him a single sentence—"I'm against that bill"—would rush to file tongue-in-cheek dispatches, proclaiming that: "President Coolidge, in a fighting mood, today served notice on Congress that he intended to combat, with all the resources at his command, the pending bill * * *"

But in the coming years, we will need a real fighting mood in the White House—a man who will not retreat in the face of pressure from his Congressional leaders—who will not let down those supporting his views on the floor . . .

The facts of the matter are that legislative leadership is not possible without party leadership, in the most political sense . . .

No President, it seems to me, can escape politics. He has not only been chosen by the nation he has been chosen by his party. And if he insists that he is "President of all the people" and should, therefore, offend none of them—if he blurs the issues and differences between the parties—if he neglects the party machinery and avoids his party's leadership—then he has not only weakened the political party as an instrument of the democratic process—he has dealt a blow to the democratic process itself.

I prefer the example of Abe Lincoln, who loved politics with the passion of a born practitioner. . . .

But the White House is not only the center of political leadership. It must be the center of moral leadership—a "bully pulpit," as Theodore Roosevelt described it. For only the President represents the national interest. And upon him alone converge all the needs and aspirations of all parts of the country, all departments of the Government, all nations of the world.

It is not enough merely to represent prevailing sentiment—to follow McKinley's practice, as described by Joe Cannon, of "keeping his ear so close to the ground he got it full of grasshoppers." We will need in the Sixties a President who is willing and able to summon his national constituency to its finest hour—to alert the people to our dangers and our opportunities—to demand of them the sacrifices that will be necessary. Despite the increasing evidence of a lost national purpose and a soft national will, F.D.R.'s words in his first inaugural still ring true: "In every dark hour of our national life, a leadership of frankness and vigor has met with that understanding and support of the people themselves which is essential to victory."

Roosevelt fulfilled the role of moral leadership. So did Wilson and Lincoln, Truman and Jackson and Teddy Roosevelt. They led the people as well as the Government—they fought for great ideals as well as bills. And the time has come to demand that kind of leadership again . . .

The next President . . . must endow that office with extraordinary strength and vision. He must act in the image of Abraham Lincoln summoning his war time cabinet to a meeting on the Emancipation Proclamation. That Cabinet had been carefully chosen to please and reflect many elements in the country. But "I have gathered you together," Lincoln said, "to hear what I have written down. I do not wish your advice about the main matter—that I have determined for myself."

And later, when he went to sign after several hours of exhausting handshaking that had left his arm weak, he said to those present: "If my name goes down in history, it will be for this act. My whole soul is in it. If my hand trembles when I sign this proclamation, all who examine the document hereafter will say: 'He hesitated.' "

But Lincoln's hand did not tremble. He did not hesitate. He did not equivocate. For he was the President of the United States.

It is in this spirit that we must go forth in the coming months and years.

Rathbun v. United States*

In Myers v. United States, *272 U.S. 52 (1926), the Court ruled that the President may remove executive officers without Congressional approval even though senatorial consent was required for their appointment. The court decided that, though this removal power was not expressly granted in the Constitution, it was supported by historical practice and implied by the general grant of executive power to the President.*

The Myers case concerned a postmastership but Chief Justice Taft, in the court opinion, advanced the dictum that the principle applied to independent regulatory commissions as well as the administrative departments. The Rathbun case over-rules this dictum while leaving intact the principle on which the Myers case rests.

Mr. Justice Sutherland delivered the opinion of the Court, saying in part:

Plaintiff brought suit in the Court of Claims against the United States to recover a sum of money alleged to be due the deceased for salary as a Federal Trade Commissioner from October 8, 1933, when the President undertook to remove him from office, to the time of his death on February 14, 1934. The court below has certified to this court two questions . . . in respect of the power of the President to make the removal. The material facts which give rise to the questions are as follows:

William E. Humphrey, the decedent, on December 10, 1931, was nominated by President Hoover to succeed himself as a member of the Federal Trade Commission, and was confirmed by the United States Senate. He was duly commissioned for a term of seven years expiring September 25, 1938; and, after taking the required oath of office, entered upon his duties. On July 25, 1933,

* 295 U.S. 602 (1935); also known as Humphrey's Executor *v.* U.S.

President Roosevelt addressed a letter to the commissioner asking for his resignation, on the ground "that the aims and purposes of the Administration with respect to the work of the Commission can be carried out most effectively with personnel of my own selection," but disclaiming any reflection upon the commissioner personally or upon his services. The commissioner replied, asking time to consult his friends. After some further correspondence upon the subject, the President on August 31, 1933, wrote the commissioner expressing the hope that the resignation would be forthcoming and saying:

"You will, I know, realize that I do not feel that your mind and my mind go along together on either the policies or the administering of the Federal Trade Commission, and, frankly, I think it is best for the people of this country that I should have a full confidence."

The commissioner declined to resign; and on October 7, 1933, the President wrote him:

"Effective as of this date you are hereby removed from the office of Commissioner of the Federal Trade Commission."

Humphrey never acquiesced in this action, but continued thereafter to insist that he was still a member of the commission, entitled to perform its duties and receive the compensation provided by law at the rate of $10,000 per annum. Upon these and other facts set forth in the certificate, which we deem it unnecessary to recite, the following questions are certified:

"1. Do the provisions of section 1 of the Federal Trade Commission Act, stating that 'any commissioner may be removed by the President for inefficiency, neglect of duty, or malfeasance in office,' restrict or limit the power of the President to remove a commissioner except upon one or more of the causes named?

"If the foregoing question is answered in the affirmative, then—

"2. If the power of the President to remove a commissioner is restricted or limited as shown by the foregoing interrogatory and the answer made thereto, is such a restriction or limitation valid under the Constitution of the United States?"

The Federal Trade Commission Act, . . . creates a

commission of five members to be appointed by the President by and with the advice and consent of the Senate, and ¶1 provides:

"Not more than three of the commissioners shall be members of the same political party. The first commissioners appointed shall continue in office for terms of three, four, five, six, and seven years, respectively, from the date of the taking effect of this Act, the term of each to be designated by the President, but their successor shall be appointed for terms of seven years, except that any person chosen to fill a vacancy shall be appointed only for the unexpired term of the commissioner whom he shall succeed. The commission shall choose a chairman from its own membership. No commissioner shall engage in any other business, vocation, or employment. Any commissioner may be removed by the President for inefficiency, neglect of duty, or malfeasance in office. . . ."

Section 5 of the act in part provides: . . .

"The commission is hereby empowered and directed to prevent persons, partnerships, or corporations, except banks, and common carriers subject to the Act to regulate commerce, from using unfair methods of competition in commerce."

In exercising this power, the commission must issue a complaint stating its charges and giving notice of hearing upon a day to be fixed. A person, partnership, or corporation proceeded against is given the right to appear at the time and place fixed and show cause why an order to cease and desist should not be issued. There is provision for intervention by others interested. If the commission finds the method of competition is one prohibited by the act, it is directed to make a report in writing stating its findings as to the facts, and to issue and cause to be served a cease and desist order. If the order is disobeyed, the commission may apply to the appropriate circuit court of appeals for its enforcement. The party subject to the order may seek and obtain a review in the circuit court of appeals in a manner provided by the act.

Section 6, among other things gives the commission wide powers of investigation in respect of certain corporations subject to the act, and in respect of other matters, upon which it must report to Congress with recommendations. Many such investigations have been made, and some have served as the basis of congressional legislation.

Section 7 provides:

"That in any suit in equity brought by or under the direction of the Attorney General as provided in the anti-trust Acts, the court may, upon the conclusion of the testimony therein, if it shall be then of opinion that the complainant is entitled to relief, refer said suit to the commission, as a master in chancery, to ascertain and report an appropriate form of decree therein. The commission shall proceed upon such notice to the parties and under such rules of procedure as the court may prescribe, and upon the coming in of such report such exceptions may be filed and such proceedings had in relation thereto as upon the report of a master in other equity causes, but the court may adopt or reject such report, in whole or in part, and enter such decree as the nature of the case may in its judgment require."

First. The question first to be considered is whether, by the provision of ¶1 of the Federal Trade Commission Act already quoted, the President's power is limited to removal for the specific causes enumerated therein. . . .

The government says the phrase "continue in office" is of no legal significance and, moreover, applies only to the first commissioners. We think it has significance. It may be that, literally, its application is restricted as suggested; but it, nevertheless, lends support to a view contrary to that of the government as to the meaning of the entire requirement in respect of tenure; for it is not easy to suppose that Congress intended to secure the first commissioners against removal except for the causes specified and deny like security to their successors. Putting this phrase aside, however, the fixing of a definite term subject to removal for cause, unless there be some counter-vailing provision or circumstances indicating the contrary, which here we are unable to find, is enough to establish the legislative intent that the term is not to be curtailed in the absence of such cause. But if the intention of Congress that no removal should be made during the specified term except for one or more of the enumerated causes were not clear upon the face of the statute, as we think it is, it would be made clear by a consideration of the character of the commission and the legislative history which accompanied and preceded the passage of the act.

The commission is to be non-partisan; and it must, from the very nature of its duties, act with entire impartiality. It is charged with the enforcement of no policy except the policy of the law. Its duties are neither political nor executive but predominantly quasi-judicial and quasi-legislative. Like the Interstate Commerce Commission, its members are called upon to exercise the trained judgment of a body of experts "appointed by law and informed by experience." . . .

The legislative reports in both houses of Congress clearly reflect the view that a fixed term was necessary to the effective and fair administration of the law . . .

The debates in both houses demonstrate that the prevailing view was that the commission was not to be "subject to anybody in the government but . . . only to the people of the United States"; free from "political domination or control" or the "probability or possibility of such a thing"; to be "separate and apart from any existing department of the government—not subject to the orders of the President." . . .

Thus, the language of the act, the legislative reports, and the general purposes of the legislation as reflected by the debates, all combine to demonstrate the Congressional intent to create a body of experts who shall gain experience by length of service—a body which shall be independent of executive authority, *except in its selection,* and free to exercise its judgment without the leave or hindrance of any other official or any department of the government. To the accomplishment of these purposes, it is clear that Congress was of opinion that length and certainty of tenure would vitally contribute. And to hold that, nevertheless, the members of the commission continue in office at the mere will of the President, might be to thwart, in large measure, the very ends which Congress sought to realize by definitely fixing the term of office.

We conclude that the intent of the act is to limit the

executive power of removal to the causes enumerated, the existence of none of which is claimed here; and we pass to the second question.

Second. To support its contention that the removal provision of ¶1, as we have just construed it, is an unconstitutional interference with the executive power of the President, the government's chief reliance is *Myers v. United States*, 272 U.S. 52 . . . Nevertheless, the narrow point actually decided was only that the President had power to remove a postmaster of the first class, without the advice and consent of the Senate as required by act of Congress. In the course of the opinion of the court, expressions occur which tend to sustain the government's contention, but these are beyond the point involved and, therefore, do not come within the rule of *stare decisis.* In so far as they are out of harmony with the views here set forth, these expressions are disapproved . . .

The office of a postmaster is so essentially unlike the office now involved that the decision in the *Myers* case cannot be accepted as controlling our decision here. A postmaster is an executive officer restricted to the performance of executive functions. He is charged with no duty at all related to either the legislative or judicial power. The actual decision in the *Myers* case finds support in the theory that such an officer is merely one of the units in the executive department and, hence, inherently subject to the exclusive and illimitable power of removal by the Chief Executive, whose subordinate and aid he is. Putting aside *dicta,* which may be followed if sufficiently persuasive but which are not controlling, the necessary reach of the decision goes far enough to include all purely executive officers. It goes no farther;—much less does it include an officer who occupies no place in the executive department and who exercises no part of the executive power vested by the Constitution in the President.

The Federal Trade Commission is an administrative body created by Congress to carry into effect legislative policies embodied in the statute in accordance with the legislative standard therein prescribed, and to perform other specified duties as a legislative or as a judicial aid. Such a body cannot in any proper sense be characterized as an arm or an eye of the executive. Its duties are performed without executive leave and, in the contemplation of the statute, must be free from executive control. In administering the provisions of the statute in respect of "unfair methods of competition"—that is to say in filling in and administering the details embodied by that general standard—the commission acts in part quasi-legislatively and in part quasi-judicially. In making investigations and reports thereon for the information of Congress under ¶6, in aid of the legislative power, it acts as a legislative agency. Under ¶7, which authorizes the commission to act as a master in chancery under rules prescribed by the court, it acts as an agency of the judiciary. To the extent that it exercises any executive function—as distinguished from executive power in the constitutional sense—it does so in the discharge and effectuation of its quasi-legislative or quasi-judicial powers, or as an agency of the legislative or judicial departments of the government.

If Congress is without authority to prescribe causes for removal of members of the trade commission and limit executive power of removal accordingly, that power at once becomes practically all-inclusive in respect of civil officers with the exception of the judiciary provided for by the Constitution. The Solicitor General, at the bar, apparently recognizing this to be true, with commendable candor, agreed that his view in respect of the removability of members of the Federal Trade Commission necessitated a like view in respect of the Interstate Commerce Commission and the Court of Claims. We are thus confronted with the serious question whether not only the members of these quasi-legislative and quasi-judicial bodies, but the judges of the legislative Court of Claims, exercising judicial power . . . continue in office only at the pleasure of the President.

We think it plain under the Constitution that illimitable power of removal is not possessed by the President in respect of officers of the character of those just named. The authority of Congress, in creating quasi-legislative or quasi-judicial agencies, to require them to act in discharge of their duties independently of executive control cannot well be doubted; and that authority includes, as an appropriate incident, power to fix the period during which they shall continue in office, and to forbid their removal except for cause in the meantime. For it is quite evident that one who holds his office only during the pleasure of another, cannot be depended upon to maintain an attitude of independence against the latter's will.

The fundamental necessity of maintaining each of the three general departments of government entirely free from the control or coercive influence, direct or indirect, of either of the others, has often been stressed and is hardly open to serious question. So much is implied in the very fact of the separation of the powers of these departments by the Constitution; and in the rule which recognizes their essential co-equality. The sound application of a principle that makes one master in his own house precludes him from imposing his control in the house of another who is master there. . . .

The power of removal here claimed for the President falls within this principle, since its coercive influence threatens the independence of a commission, which is not only wholly disconnected from the executive department, but which, as already fully appears, was created by Congress as a means of carrying into operation legislative and judicial powers, and as an agency of the legislative and judicial departments.

In the light of the question now under consideration, we have reexamined the precedents referred to in the *Myers* case, and find nothing in them to justify a conclusion contrary to that which we have reached. . . .

The result of what we now have said is this: Whether the power of the President to remove an officer shall prevail over the authority of Congress to condition the power by fixing a definite term and precluding a removal except for cause, will depend upon the character of the office; the *Myers* decision, affirming the power of the President alone to make the removal, is confined to purely executive officers; and as to officers of the kind here under consideration, we hold that no removal can be made during the prescribed term for which the officer is appointed, except for one or more of the causes named in the applicable statute.

To the extent that, between the decision in the *Myers* case, which sustains the unrestrictable power of the President to remove purely executive officers, and our present decision that such power does not extend to an office such as that here involved, there shall remain a field of doubt, we leave such cases as may fall within it for future consideration and determination as they may arise.

In accordance with the foregoing, the questions submitted are answered.

Question No. 1, Yes.
Question No. 2, Yes.

YOUNGSTOWN SHEET AND TUBE CO. v. SAWYER *

After the war in Korea had become stalemated but before agreement was reached on an armistice, a dispute came to a head between the United Steel Workers of America and the steel manufacturers. The union announced its intention to strike in December 1951 and, after a delay in which efforts to reach a settlement failed, again on April 9, 1952.

As a last recourse to avoid the closing of the mills during the war crisis, President Truman ordered Secretary of Commerce Sawyer to seize and operate the mills. The steel companies sought to block the seizures through court injunction on the grounds that the President lacked constitutional sanction for such a step.

Acting with unaccustomed dispatch, the Court bypassed the Court of Appeals, placed the case on its docket on May 3, heard arguments on May 12, and handed down its decision on June 2. The Court divided in favor of the steel companies, six to three, with seven justices writing opinions.

* 343 U.S. 579 (1952). For an interesting and useful study in depth of this case as an example of the operation of the American judicial system in dealing with a constitutional law case, see Alan F. Westin, *The Anatomy of a Constitutional Law Case,* Macmillan, New York, 1958, 183 pp.

Mr. Justice Black delivered the opinion of the Court, saying in part:

We are asked to decide whether the President was acting within his constitutional power when he issued an order directing the Secretary of Commerce to take possession of and operate most of the Nation's steel mills. The mill owners argue that the President's order amounts to lawmaking, a legislative function which the Constitution has expressly confided to the Congress and not to the President. The Government's position is that the order was made on findings of the President that his action was necessary to avert a national catastrophe which would inevitably result from a stoppage of steel production, and that in meeting this grave emergency the President was acting within the aggregate of his constitutional powers as the Nation's Chief Executive and the Commander in Chief of the Armed Forces of the United States. . . .

The President's power, if any, to issue the order must stem either from an act of Congress or from the Constitution itself. There is no statute that expressly authorizes the President to take possession of property as he did here. Nor is there any act of Congress to which our attention has been directed from which such a power can fairly be implied. Indeed, we do not understand the Government to rely on statutory authorization for this seizure. There are two statutes which do authorize the President to take both personal and real property under certain conditions. However, the Government admits that these conditions were not met and that the President's order was not rooted in either of the statutes . . .

Moreover, the use of the seizure technique to solve labor disputes in order to prevent work stoppages was not only unauthorized by any congressional enactment; prior to this controversy, Congress had refused to adopt that method of settling labor disputes. When the Taft-Hartley Act was under consideration in 1947, Congress rejected an amendment which would have authorized such governmental seizures in cases of emergency. Apparently it was thought that the technique of seizure, like that of compulsory arbitration, would interfere with the process of collective bargaining. Consequently, the plan Congress adopted in that Act did not provide for seizure under any circumstances. Instead, the plan sought to bring about settlements by use of the customary devices of mediation, conciliation, investigation by boards of inquiry, and public reports. In some instances temporary injunctions were authorized to provide cooling-off periods. All this failing, unions were left free to strike after a secret vote by employees as to whether they wished to accept their employers' final settlement offer.

It is clear that if the President had authority to issue the order he did, it must be found in some provision of the Constitution. And it is not claimed that express constitutional language grants this power to the President. The contention is that presidential power should be implied from the aggregate of his powers under the Constitution. Particular reliance is placed on provisions in Article II which say that "The executive Power shall be vested in a President . . ."; that "he shall take Care that the Laws be faithfully executed"; and that he "shall be Commander in Chief of the Army and Navy of the United States."

The order cannot properly be sustained as an exercise of the President's military power as Commander in Chief of the Armed Forces. The Governmental attempts to do so by citing a number of cases upholding broad powers in military commanders engaged in day-to-day fighting in a theater of war. Such cases need not concern us here. Even though "theater of war" be an expanding concept, we cannot with faithfulness to our constitutional system hold that the Commander in Chief of the Armed Forces has the ultimate power as such to take possession of private property in order to keep labor disputes from stopping production. This is a job for the Nation's lawmakers, not for its military authorities.

Nor can the seizure order be sustained because of the several constitutional provisions that grant executive power to the President. In the framework of our Constitution, the President's power to see that the laws are faithfully executed refutes the idea that he is to be a lawmaker. The Constitution limits his functions in the lawmaking process to the recommending of laws he thinks wise and the vetoing of laws he thinks bad. And the Constitution is neither silent nor equivocal about who shall make laws which the President is to execute. The first section of the first article says that "All legislative Powers herein granted shall be vested in a Congress of the United States. . . ." After granting many powers to the Congress, Article I goes on to provide that Congress may "make all Laws which shall be necessary and proper for carrying into Execution the foregoing Powers, and all other Powers vested by this Constitution in the Government of the United States, or in any Department or Officer thereof."

The President's order does not direct that a congressional policy be executed in a manner prescribed by Congress—it directs that a presidential policy be executed in a manner prescribed by the President. The preamble of the order itself, like that of many statutes, sets out reasons why the President believes certain policies should be adopted, proclaims these policies as rules of conduct to be followed, and again, like a statute, authorizes a government official to promulgate additional rules and regulations consistent with the policy proclaimed and needed to carry that policy into execution. The power of Congress to adopt such public policies as those proclaimed by the order is beyond question. It can authorize the taking of private property for public use. It can make laws regulating the relationships between employers and employees, prescribing rules designed to settle labor disputes, and fixing wages and working conditions in certain fields of our economy. The Constitution does not subject this lawmaking power of Congress to presidential or military supervision or control.

It is said that other Presidents without congressional authority have taken possession of private business enterprises in order to settle labor disputes. But even if this be true, Congress has not thereby lost its exclusive constitutional authority to make laws necessary and proper to carry out the powers vested by the Constitution "in the Government of the United States, or any Department or Officer thereof."

The Founders of this Nation entrusted the lawmaking

power to the Congress alone in both good and bad times. It would do no good to recall the historical events, the fears of power and the hopes for freedom that lay behind their choice. Such a review would but confirm our holding that this seizure order cannot stand.

[*The case was decided, 6 to 3. Each of the other five majority justices submitted concurring opinions and Chief Justice Vinson submitted a dissenting opinion to which Justices Reed and Minton subscribed.—Ed. note.*]

— 5 —

THE SUPREME COURT

FEDERALIST NO. 78

By Alexander Hamilton

The following essay is most significant as an exposition of the intentions of one of the Framers regarding the role of the United States Supreme Court in declaring action by Congress or the President void because unconstitutional—that is, the power of judicial review.

We proceed now to an examination of the judiciary department of the proposed government.

In unfolding the defects of the existing Confederation, the utility and necessity of a federal judicature have been clearly pointed out. It is the less necessary to recapitulate the considerations there urged, as the propriety of the institution in the abstract is not disputed; the only questions which have been raised being relative to the manner of constituting it, and to its extent. To these points, therefore, our observations shall be confined.

The manner of constituting it seems to embrace these several objects: 1st. The mode of appointing the judges. 2d. The tenure by which they are to hold their places. 3d. The partition of the judiciary authority between different courts, and their relations to each other.

First. As to the mode of appointing the judges; this is the same with that of appointing the officers of the Union in general, and has been so fully discussed in the two last numbers, that nothing can be said here which would not be useless repetition.

Second. As to the tenure by which the judges are to hold their places: this chiefly concerns their duration in office; the provisions for their support; the precautions for their responsibility.

According to the plan of the convention, all judges who may be appointed by the United States are to hold their offices *during good behavior;* which is conformable to the most approved of the State constitutions, and among the rest, to that of this State. Its propriety having been drawn into question by the adversaries of that plan, is no light symptom of the rage for objection, which disorders their imaginations and judgments. The standard of good behavior for the continuance in office of the judicial magistracy, is certainly one of the most valuable of the modern improvements in the practice of government. In a monarchy it is an excellent barrier to the despotism of the prince; in a republic it is a no less excellent barrier to the encroachments and oppressions of the representative body. And it is the best expedient which can be devised in any government, to secure a steady, upright, and impartial administration of the laws.

Whoever attentively considers the different departments of power must perceive, that, in a government in which they are separated from each other, the judiciary, from the nature of its functions, will always be the least dangerous to the political rights of the Constitution; because it will be least in a capacity to annoy or injure them. The Executive not only dispenses the honors, but holds the sword of the community. The legislature not only commands the purse, but prescribes the rules by which the duties and rights of every citizen are to be regulated. The judiciary, on the contrary, has no influence over either the sword or the purse; no direction either of the strength or of the wealth of the society; and can take no active resolution whatever. It may truly be said to have neither FORCE nor WILL, but merely judgment; and must ultimately depend upon the aid of the executive arm even for the efficacy of its judgments.

This simple view of the matter suggests several important consequences. It proves incontestably, that the judiciary is beyond comparison the weakest of the three departments of power;[1] that it can never attack with success either of the other two; and that all possible care is requisite to enable it to defend itself against their attacks. It equally proves, that though individual oppression may now and then proceed from the courts of justice, the general liberty of the people can never be endangered from that quarter; I mean so long as the judiciary remains truly distinct from both the legislature and the Executive. For I agree, that "there is no liberty, if the power of judging be not separated from the legislative and executive powers."[2] And it proves, in the last place, that as liberty can have nothing to fear from the judiciary alone, but would have every thing to fear from its union with either of the other departments; that as all the effects of such a union must ensue from a dependence of the former on the latter, notwithstanding a nominal and apparent separation; that as, from the natural feebleness of the judiciary, it is in continual jeopardy of being overpowered, awed, or influenced by its coördinate branches; and that as nothing can contribute so much to its firmness and independence as permanency in office, this quality may therefore be justly regarded as an indispensable ingredient in its constitution, and, in a great measure, as the citadel of the public justice and the public security.

The complete independence of the courts of justice is peculiarly essential in a limited Constitution. By a limited Constitution, I understand one which contains certain specified exceptions to the legislative authority; such, for instance, as that it shall pass no bills of attainder, no *ex-post-facto* laws, and the like. Limitations of this kind can be preserved in practice no other way than through the medium of courts of justice, whose duty it must be to declare all acts contrary to the manifest tenor of the Constitution void. Without this, all the reservations of particular rights or privileges would amount to nothing.

Some perplexity respecting the rights of the courts to

[1] The celebrated Montesquieu, speaking of them, says: "Of the three powers above mentioned, the judiciary is next to nothing."—"Spirit of Laws," vol. i., page 186.—PUBLIUS

[2] *Idem,* page 181.—PUBLIUS

pronounce legislative acts void, because contrary to the constitution, has arisen from an imagination that the doctrine would imply a superiority of the judiciary to the legislative power. It is urged that the authority which can declare the acts of another void, must necessarily be superior to the one whose acts may be declared void. As this doctrine is of great importance in all the American constitutions, a brief discussion of the ground on which it rests cannot be unacceptable.

There is no position which depends on clearer principles, than that every act of a delegated authority, contrary to the tenor of the commission under which it is exercised, is void. No legislative act, therefore, contrary to the Constitution, can be valid. To deny this, would be to affirm, that the deputy is greater than his principal; that the servant is above his master; that the representatives of the people are superior to the people themselves; that men acting by virtue of powers, may do not only what their powers do not authorize, but what they forbid.

If it be said that the legislative body are themselves the constitutional judges of their own powers, and that the construction they put upon them is conclusive upon the other departments, it may be answered, that this cannot be the natural presumption, where it is not to be collected from any particular provisions in the Constitution. It is not otherwise to be supposed, that the Constitution could intend to enable the representatives of the people to substitute their *will* to that of their constituents. It is far more rational to suppose, that the courts were designed to be an intermediate body between the people and the legislature, in order, among other things, to keep the latter within the limits assigned to their authority. The interpretation of the laws is the proper and peculiar province of the courts. A constitution is, in fact, and must be regarded by the judges, as a fundamental law. It therefore belongs to them to ascertain its meaning, as well as the meaning of any particular act proceeding from the legislative body. If there should happen to be an irreconcilable variance between the two, that which has the superior obligation and validity ought, of course, to be preferred; or, in other words, the Constitution ought to be preferred to the statute, the intention of the people to the intention of their agents.

Nor does this conclusion by any means suppose a superiority of the judicial to the legislative power. It only supposes that the power of the people is superior to both; and that where the will of the legislature, declared in its statutes, stands in opposition to that of the people, declared in the Constitution, the judges ought to be governed by the latter rather than the former. They ought to regulate their decisions by the fundamental laws, rather than by those which are not fundamental.

This exercise of judicial discretion, in determining between two contradictory laws, is exemplified in a familiar instance. It not uncommonly happens, that there are two statutes existing at one time, clashing in whole or in part with each other, and neither of them containing any repealing clause or expression. In such a case, it is the province of the courts to liquidate and fix their meaning and operation. So far as they can, by any fair construction, be reconciled to each other, reason and law conspire to dictate that this should be done; where this is impracticable, it becomes a matter of necessity to give effect to one, in exclusion of the other. The rule which has obtained in the courts for determining their relative validity is, that the last in order of time shall be preferred to the first. But this is a mere rule of construction, not derived from any positive law, but from the nature and reason of the thing. It is a rule not enjoined upon the courts by legislative provision, but adopted by themselves, as consonant to truth and propriety, for the direction of their conduct as interpreters of the law. They thought it reasonable, that between the interfering acts of an *equal* authority, that which was the last indication of its will should have the preference.

But in regard to the interfering acts of a superior and subordinate authority, of an original and derivative power, the nature and reason of the thing indicate the converse of that rule as proper to be followed. They teach us that the prior act of a superior ought to be preferred to the subsequent act of an inferior and subordinate authority; and that accordingly, whenever a particular statute contravenes the Constitution, it will be the duty of the judicial tribunals to adhere to the latter and disregard the former.

It can be of no weight to say that the courts, on the pretence of a repugnancy, may substitute their own pleasure to the constitutional intentions of the legislature. This might as well happen in the case of two contradictory statutes; or it might as well happen in every adjudication upon any single statute. The courts must declare the sense of the law; and if they should be disposed to exercise WILL instead of JUDGMENT, the consequence would equally be the substitution of their pleasure to that of the legislative body. The observation, if it prove any thing, would prove that there ought to be no judges distinct from that body.

If, then, the courts of justice are to be considered as the bulwarks of a limited Constitution against legislative encroachments, this consideration will afford a strong argument for the permanent tenure of judicial offices, since nothing will contribute so much as this to that independent spirit in the judges which must be essential to the faithful performance of so arduous a duty.

This independence of the judges is equally requisite to guard the Constitution and the rights of individuals from the effects of those ill humors, which the arts of designing men, or the influence of particular conjunctures, sometimes disseminate among the people themselves, and which, though they speedily give place to better information, and more deliberate reflection, have a tendency, in the meantime, to occasion dangerous innovations in the government, and serious oppressions of the minor party in the community. Though I trust the friends of the proposed Constitution will never concur with its enemies,[3] in questioning that fundamental principle of republican government, which admits the right of the people to alter or abolish the established Constitution, whenever they find it inconsistent with their happiness, yet it is not to be inferred from this principle, that the representatives of the people, whenever a momentary inclination happens to lay hold of a majority of their constituents, in-

[3] *Vide* "Protest of the Minority of the Convention of Pennsylvania," Martin's Speech, etc.—PUBLIUS

compatible with the provisions in the existing Constitution, would, on that account, be justifiable in a violation of those provisions; or that the courts would be under a greater obligation to connive at infractions in this shape, than when they had proceeded wholly from the cabals of the representative body. Until the people have, by some solemn and authoritative act, annulled or changed the established form, it is binding upon themselves collectively, as well as individually; and no presumption, or even knowledge, of their sentiments, can warrant their representatives in a departure from it, prior to such an act. But it is easy to see, that it would require an uncommon portion of fortitude in the judges to do their duty as faithful guardians of the Constitution, where legislative invasions of it had been instigated by the major voice of the community.

But it is not with a view to infractions of the Constitution only, that the independence of the judges may be an essential safeguard against the effects of occasional ill humors in the society. These sometimes extend no farther than to the injury of the private rights of particular classes of citizens, by unjust and partial laws. Here also the firmness of the judicial magistracy is of vast importance in mitigating the severity and confining the operation of such laws. It not only serves to moderate the immediate mischiefs of those which may have been passed but it operates as a check upon the legislative body in passing them; who, perceiving that obstacles to the success of iniquitous intention are to be expected from the scruples of the courts, are in a manner compelled, by the very motives of the injustice they meditate, to qualify their attempts. This is a circumstance calculated to have more influence upon the character of our governments, than but few may be aware of. The benefits of the integrity and moderation of the judiciary have already been felt in more States than one; and though they may have displeased those whose sinister expectations they may have disappointed, they must have commanded the esteem and applause of all the virtuous and disinterested. Considerate men, of every description, ought to prize whatever will tend to beget or fortify that temper in the courts; as no man can be sure that he may not be to-morrow the victim of a spirit of injustice, by which he may be a gainer to-day. And every man must now feel, that the inevitable tendency of such a spirit is to sap the foundations of public and private confidence, and to introduce in its stead universal distrust and distress.

That inflexible and uniform adherence to the rights of the Constitution, and of individuals, which we perceive to be indispensable in the courts of justice, can certainly not be expected from judges who hold their offices by a temporary commission. Periodical appointments, however regulated, or by whomsoever made, would, in some way or other, be fatal to their necessary independence. If the power of making them was committed either to the Executive or legislature, there would be danger of an improper complaisance to the branch which possessed it; if to both, there would be an unwillingness to hazard the displeasure of either; if to the people, or to persons chosen by them for the special purpose, there would be too great a disposition to consult popularity, to justify a reliance that nothing would be consulted but the Constitution and the laws.

There is yet a further and a weightier reason for the permanency of the judicial offices, which is deducible from the nature of the qualifications they require. It has been frequently remarked, with great propriety, that a voluminous code of laws is one of the inconveniences necessarily connected with the advantages of a free government. To avoid an arbitrary discretion in the courts, it is indispensable that they should be bound down by strict rules and precedents, which serve to define and point out their duty in every particular case that comes before them; and it will readily be conceived from the variety of controversies which grow out of the folly and wickedness of mankind, that the records of those precedents must unavoidably swell to a very considerable bulk, and must demand long and laborious study to acquire a competent knowledge of them. Hence it is, that there can be but few men in the society who will have sufficient skill in the laws to qualify them for the stations of judges. And making the proper deductions for the ordinary depravity of human nature, the number must be still smaller of those who unite the requisite integrity with the requisite knowledge. These considerations apprise us, that the government can have no great option between fit character; and that a temporary duration in office, which would naturally discourage such characters from quitting a lucrative line of practice to accept a seat on the bench, would have a tendency to throw the administration of justice into hands less able, and less well qualified, to conduct it with utility and dignity. In the present circumstances of this country, and in those in which it is likely to be for a long time to come, the disadvantages on this score would be greater than they may at first sight appear; but it must be confessed, that they are far inferior to those which present themselves under the other aspects of the subject.

Upon the whole, there can be no room to doubt that the convention acted wisely in copying from the models of those constitutions which have established *good behavior* as the tenure of their judicial offices, in point of duration; and that so far from being blamable on this account, their plan would have been inexcusably defective, if it had wanted this important feature of good government. The experience of Great Britain affords an illustrious comment on the excellence of the institution.

PUBLIUS

MARBURY v. MADISON, 1803 *

In 1801 with the relinquishment by the Federalists of the national administration, Secretary of State John Marshall left office. On his last day in office he signed the commissions of a number of "midnight appointees" to judicial offices. One of the commissions he signed was his own appointment as Chief Justice. One he signed but failed to deliver was that of William Marbury, Justice of the Peace.

The new secretary of state, James Madison, refused to deliver the commission and Marbury sued for a writ of mandamus requiring its delivery. The new administration served notice that it would not deliver the commission even if so ordered by the Court.

Marshall resolved the predicament by ruling that the court had no power to issue such writs because the

* 1 Cranch (U.S.) 137 (1803).

portion of the Judiciary Act of 1789 which purported to confer this power on the Court was unconstitutional because it expanded the original jurisdiction of the court beyond that conferred by the Constitution.

In some respects Marbury v. Madison *has the appearance of a "cooked-up" case, but it established the principle of judicial review of legislation and executive acts for constitutionality as a permanent part of American constitutional law.*

Marshall, Chief Justice, delivered the opinion of the Court, saying in part:

The question, whether an act, repugnant to the constitution, can become the law of the land, is a question deeply interesting to the United States; but, happily, not of an intricacy proportioned to its interest. It seems only necessary to recognize certain principles, supposed to have been long and well established, to decide it.

That the people have an original right to establish, for their future government, such principles, as, in their opinion, shall most conduce to their own happiness is the basis on which the whole American fabric has been erected. The exercise of this original right is a very great exertion; nor can it, nor ought it, to be frequently repeated. The principles, therefore, so established, are deemed fundamental. And as the authority from which they proceed is supreme, and can seldom act, they are designed to be permanent.

This original and supreme will organizes the government, and assigns to different departments their respective powers. It may either stop here, or establish certain limits not to be transcended by those departments.

The government of the United States is of the latter description. The powers of the legislature are defined and limited; and that those limits may not be mistaken, or forgotten, the constitution is written. To what purpose are powers limited, and to what purpose is that limitation committed to writing, if these limits may, at any time, be passed by those intended to be restrained? The distinction between a government with limited and unlimited powers is abolished, if those limits do not confine the persons on whom they are imposed, and if acts prohibited and acts allowed, are of equal obligation. It is a proposition too plain to be contested, that the constitution controls any legislative act repugnant to it; or, that the legislature may alter the constitution by an ordinary act.

Between these alternatives there is no middle ground. The constitution is either a superior paramount law, unchangeable by ordinary means, or it is on a level with ordinary legislative acts, and, like other acts, is alterable when the legislature shall please to alter it.

If the former part of the alternative be true, then a legislative act contrary to the constitution is not law: if the latter part be true, then written constitutions are absurd attempts, on the part of the people, to limit a power in its own nature illimitable.

Certainly all those who have framed written constitutions contemplate them as forming the fundamental and paramount law of the nation, and, consequently, the theory of every such government must be, that an act of the legislature, repugnant to the constitution, is void.

This theory is essentially attached to a written constitution, and, is consequently, to be considered, by this court, as one of the fundamental principles of our society. It is not therefore to be lost sight of in the further consideration of this subject.

If an act of the legislature, repugnant to the constitution, is void, does it, notwithstanding its invalidity, bind the courts, and oblige them to give it effect? Or, in other words, though it be not law, does it constitute a rule as operative as if it was a law? This would be to overthrow in fact what was established in theory; and would seem, at first view, an absurdity too gross to be insisted on. It shall, however, receive a more attentive consideration.

It is emphatically the province and duty of the judicial department to say what the law is. Those who apply the rule to particular cases, must of necessity expound and interpret that rule. If two laws conflict with each other, the courts must decide on the operation of each.

So if a law be in opposition to the constitution; if both the law and the constitution apply to a particular case, so that the court must either decide that case conformably to the law, disregarding the constitution; or conformably to the constitution, disregarding the law; the court must determine which of these conflicting rules governs the case. This is of the very essence of judicial duty.

If, then, the courts are to regard the constitution, and the constitution is superior to any ordinary act of the legislature, the constitution and not such ordinary act, must govern the case to which they both apply.

Those, then, who controvert the principle that the constitution is to be considered, in court, as a paramount law, are reduced to the necessity of maintaining that courts must close their eyes on the constitution, and see only the law.

This doctrine would subvert the very foundation of all written constitutions. It would declare that an act which, according to the principles and theory of our government, is entirely void, is yet, in practice, completely obligatory. It would declare that if the legislature shall do what is expressly forbidden, such act, notwithstanding the express prohibition, is in reality effectual. It would be given to the legislature a practical and real omnipotence, with the same breath which professes to restrict their powers within narrow limits. It is prescribing limits, and declaring that those limits may be passed at pleasure.

That it thus reduces to nothing what we have deemed the greatest improvement on political institutions, a written constitution, would of itself be sufficient, in America, where written constitutions have been viewed with so much reverence, for rejecting the construction. But the peculiar expressions of the constitution of the United States furnish additional arguments in favour of its rejection.

The judicial power of the United States is extended to all cases arising under the constitution.

Could it be the intention of those who gave this power, to say that in using it the constitution should not be looked into? That a case arising under the constitution should be decided without examining the instrument under which it arises?

This is too extravagant to be maintained.

In some cases, then, the constitution must be looked into by the judges. And if they can open it at all, what part of it are they forbidden to read or to obey?

There are many other parts of the constitution which serve to illustrate this subject.

It is declared that "no tax or duty shall be laid on articles exported from any state." Suppose a duty on the export of cotton, of tobacco, or of flour; and a suit instituted to recover it. Ought judgment to be rendered in such a case? ought the judges to close their eyes on the constitution, and only see the law?

The constitution declares "that no bill of attainder or ex post facto law shall be passed."

If, however, such a bill should be passed, and a person should be prosecuted under it; must the court condemn to death those victims whom the constitution endeavors to preserve?

"No person," says the constitution, "shall be convicted of treason unless on the testimony of two witnesses to the same overt act, or on confession in open court."

Here the language of the constitution is addressed especially to the courts. It prescribes, directly for them, a rule of evidence not to be departed from. If the legislature should change that rule, and declare one witness, or a confession out of court, sufficient for conviction, must the constitutional principle yield to the legislative act?

From these, and many other selections which might be made, it is apparent that the framers of the constitution contemplated that instrument as a rule for the government of courts, as well as of the legislature.

Why otherwise does it direct the judges to take an oath to support it? This oath certainly applies in an especial manner, to their conduct in their official character. How immoral to impose it on them, if they were to be used as the instruments, and the knowing instruments, for violating what they swear to support!

The oath of office, too, imposed by the legislature, is completely demonstrative of the legislative opinion on this subject. It is in these words: "I do solemnly swear that I will administer justice without respect to persons, and do equal right to the poor and to the rich; and that I will faithfully and impartially discharge all the duties incumbent on me as   , according to the best of my abilities and understanding agreeably to the constitution and laws of the United States."

Why does a judge swear to discharge his duties agreeably to the constitution of the United States, if that constitution forms no rule for his government? if it is closed upon him, and cannot be inspected by him?

If such be the real state of things, this is worse than solemn mockery. To prescribe, or to take this oath, becomes equally a crime.

It is also not entirely unworthy of observation, that in declaring what shall be the supreme law of the land, the constitution itself is first mentioned; and not the laws of the United States generally, but those only which shall be made in pursuance of the constitution, have that rank.

Thus, the particular phraseology of the constitution of the United States confirms and strengthens the principle, supposed to be essential to all written constitutions, that a law repugnant to the constitution is void; and that courts, as well as other departments, are bound by that instrument.

COLEGROVE *et al.* v. GREEN *et al.**

The seats in the House of Representatives are reapportioned after each census. Congress requires that they be filled from single-member districts, but it permits the states to determine the boundaries of the districts. Some congressional districts have been drawn up deliberately in such a way as to give to one party an electoral advantage. This practice is called "gerrymander." In other cases, the state legislature does not remap districts despite population changes that have produced inequalities in the size of the districts.

The Colegrove case involves the latter situation. Illinois districts had not been redrawn since 1901. By 1946 one district in Chicago had a population of 914,053 and another had only 112,116 inhabitants.

The "political question" principle on which the Colegrove decision rests has been applied in a variety of other situations where the Court felt that judicial remedy was inappropriate or infeasible. One early example was Luther v. Borden, *7 Howard 1 (1849), in which the court refused to decide which of two competing govern-*

* 328 U.S. 549 (1946).

ments in Rhode Island was legitimate. In other cases it has refused on these grounds to pass judgment on the exercise of Presidential powers in foreign affairs, on the "republican" form of a state government, and on the validity of constitutional amendment ratifications. In each instance, it has ruled that decisions on these questions must be made by Congress or the President and are not subject to judicial review.

It is a little difficult to find the common element in "political questions" that distinguishes them from questions the Court will decide, except that they generally involve the exercise of discretionary powers granted one or the other of the political branches of government. The Court apparently is unwilling to examine for soundness decisions made in pursuance of such powers.

Mr. Justice Frankfurter announced the judgment of the Court . . .

Appellants . . . are three qualified voters in Illinois districts which have much larger populations than other Illinois Congressional districts. They brought this suit against the Governor, the Secretary of State, and the Auditor of the State of Illinois, as members *ex officio* of the Illinois Primary Certifying Board, to restrain them, in effect, from taking proceedings for an election in November 1946, under the provisions of Illinois law governing Congressional districts . . . Formally, the appellants asked for a decree, with its incidental relief . . . declaring these provisions to be invalid because they violated various provisions of the United States Constitution and ¶3 of the Reapportionment Act of August 8, 1911 . . . in that by reason of subsequent changes in population the Congressional districts for the election of Representatives in the Congress created by the Illinois Laws of 1901 . . . lacked compactness of territory and approximate equality of population. The District Court . . . dismissed the complaint . . .

We are of opinion that the appellants ask of this Court what is beyond its competence to grant. This is one of those demands on judicial power which cannot be met by verbal fencing about "jurisdiction." It must be resolved by considerations on the basis of which this Court, from time to time, has refused to intervene in controversies. It has refused to do so because due regard for the effective working of our Government revealed this issue to be of a peculiarly political nature and therefore not meet for judicial determination.

This is not an action to recover for damage because of the discriminatory exclusion of a plaintiff from rights enjoyed by other citizens. The basis for the suit is not a private wrong, but a wrong suffered by Illinois as a polity . . . In effect this is an appeal to the federal courts to reconstruct the electoral process of Illinois in order that it may be adequately represented in the councils of the Nation. Because the Illinois legislature has failed to revise its Congressional Representative districts in order to reflect great changes, during more than a generation, in the distribution of its population, we are asked to do this, as it were, for Illinois.

Of course no court can affirmatively re-map the Illinois districts so as to bring them more in conformity with the standards of fairness for a representative system. At best we could only declare the existing electoral system invalid. The result would be to leave Illinois undistricted and to bring into operation, if the Illinois legislature chose not to act, the choice of members for the House of Representatives on a state-wide ticket. The last stage may be worse than the first. The upshot of judicial action may defeat the vital political principle which led Congress, more than a hundred years ago, to require districting . . . Assuming acquiescence on the part of the authorities of Illinois in the selection of its Representatives by a mode that defies the direction of Congress for selection by districts, the House of Representatives may not acquiesce. In the exercise of its power to judge the qualifications of its own members, the House may reject a delegation of Representatives-at-large . . . Nothing is clearer than that this controversy concerns matters that bring courts into immediate and active relations with party contests. From the determination of such issues this Court has traditionally held aloof. It is hostile to a democratic system to involve the judiciary in the politics of the people. And it is not less pernicious if such judicial intervention in an essentially political contest be dressed up in the abstract phrases of the law.

The appellants urge with great zeal that the conditions of which they complain are grave evils and offend public morality. The Constitution of the United States gives ample power to provide against these evils. But due regard for the Constitution as a viable system precludes judicial correction. Authority for dealing with such problems resides elsewhere. Article I, 4 of the Constitution provides that "The Times, Places and Manner of holding Elections for . . . Representatives, shall be prescribed in each State by the Legislature thereof; but the Congress may at any time by Law make or alter such Regulations. . . ." The short of it is that the Constitution has conferred upon Congress exclusive authority to secure fair representation by the States in the popular House and left to that House determination whether States have fulfilled their responsibility. If Congress failed in exercising its powers, whereby standards of fairness are offended, the remedy ultimately lies with the people. Whether Congress faithfully discharges its duty or not, the subject has been committed to the exclusive control of Congress. An aspect of government from which the judiciary, in view of what is involved, has been excluded by the clear intention of the Constitution cannot be entered by the federal courts because Congress may have been in default in exacting from States obedience to its mandate.

The one stark fact that emerges from a study of the history of Congressional apportionment is its embroilment in politics, in the sense of party contests and party interests . . . Throughout our history, whatever may have been the controlling Apportionment Act, the most glaring disparities have prevailed as to the contours and the population of districts. . . .

Mr. Justice Jackson took no part in the consideration or decision of this case.

INDEX

Italics indicate citations to works; **bold face type** indicate works.